Piano / Vocal / Guitar

SONGS
PROTEST

IMAGINE

GET UP
STAND UP!

POWER
TO THE
PEOPLE

GIVE
PEACE
A CHANCE

We Shall
OVERCOME

ISBN 978-1-4950-7626-8

HAL•LEONARD®
7777 W. BLUEMOUND RD. P.O. BOX 13819 MILWAUKEE, WI 53213

Visit Hal Leonard Online at
www.halleonard.com

BLOWIN' IN THE WIND

Words and Music by
BOB DYLAN

Moderately fast

How man-y roads ___
how man-y years ___
how man-y times ___

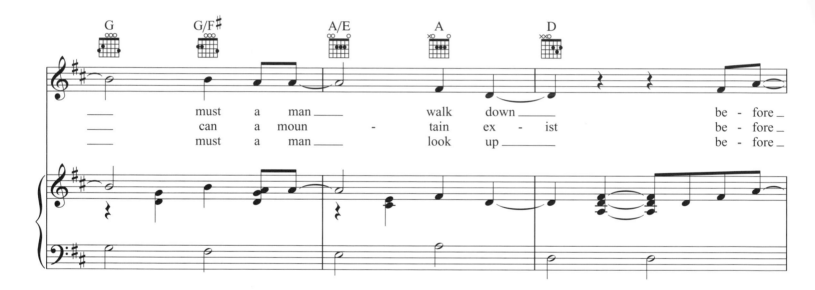

___ must a man ___ walk down ___ be-fore ___
___ can a moun - tain ex - ist be-fore ___
___ must a man ___ look up ___ be-fore ___

___ you call ___ him a man? ___
it is washed ___ to the sea? ___
he can see ___ the sky? ___

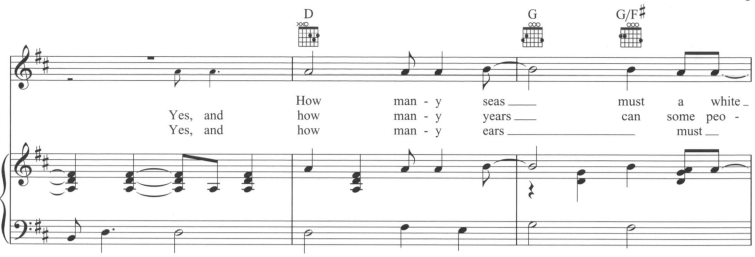

How man-y seas _____ must a white _
Yes, and how man-y years _____ can some peo -
Yes, and how man-y ears _____ must _

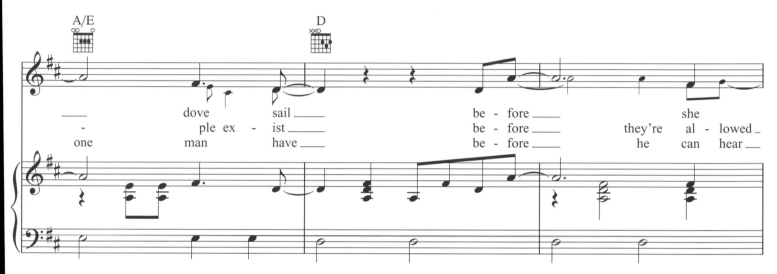

_____ dove sail _____ be - fore _____ she
- ple ex - ist _____ be - fore _____ they're al - lowed _
one man have _____ be - fore _____ he can hear _

sleeps in the sand? ___
_____ to be free? ___
_____ peo - ple cry? ___

Yes, and how _
Yes, and how _
Yes, and how _

_____ man - y times _____ must the can - non - balls
man - y times _____ can a man _____ turn _ his
man - y deaths _____ will it take _____ 'til _____ he

fly ___ be - fore ___ they are for - ev - er banned? ___
head and pre - tend ___ that he just ___ does - n't see? ___
knows that ___ too man - y peo - ple have died? ___

The an - swer, my friend, _

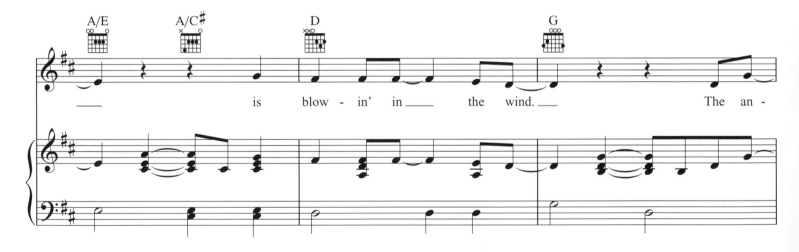

is blow - in' in ___ the wind. ___ The an -

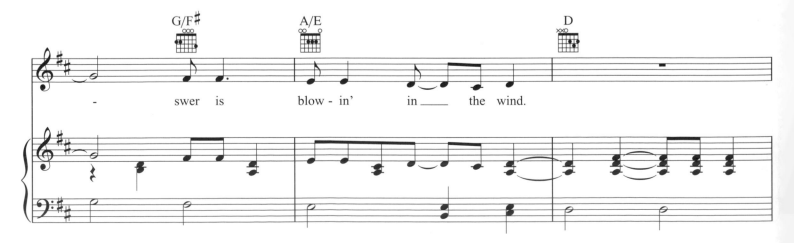

- swer is blow - in' in ___ the wind.

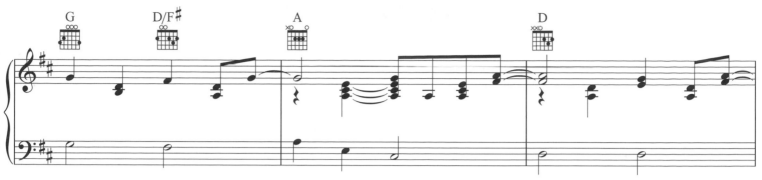

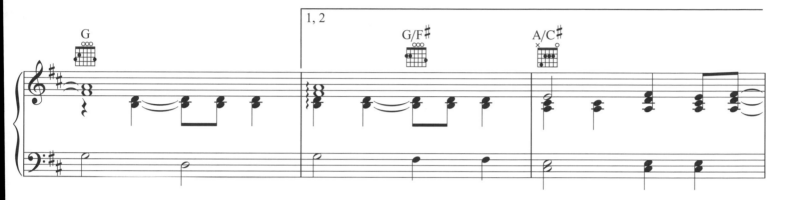

(2.,3.) Yes,   and

THE BOXER

Words and Music by
PAUL SIMON

*Recorded a half step lower.

hears ____ what he wants to hear __ and dis - re - gards __ the rest. Mm, ____

____ mm. ____

____

When I left ____ my home _ and my

Instrumental solo

fam - i - ly I was no more than a boy ____ in the com - pa - ny ____ of

stran - gers in the qui - et of the rail - way sta - tion, run - ning scared,

lay - ing low, seek - ing out___ the poor - er quar-

- ters where the rag - ged peo - ple go,___ look-ing for___ the plac - es on-

- ly they would know. *Solo ends* Lie - la - lie,___

lie - la - lie - la - lie - la - lie, ____ lie - la - lie, ____

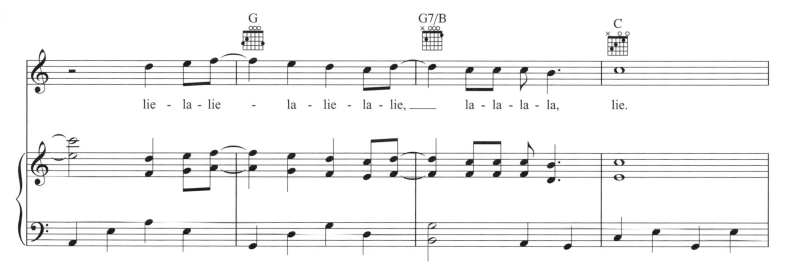

lie - la - lie - la - lie - la - lie, ____ la - la - la - la, lie.

To Coda

Ask - ing on - ly work-man's

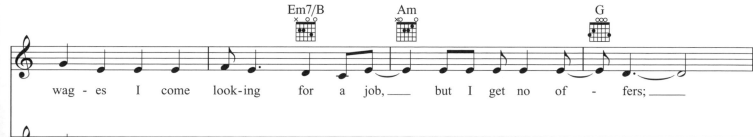

wag - es I come look-ing for a job, ____ but I get no of - fers; ____

just a come on from the whores _ on Sev-enth Av - e - nue. ___

— I do de-clare, _ there were times _ when I ___ was so _

— lone-some, I took some com-fort there. _ Ooh, la - la - la - la - la - la - la. _

D.S. al Coda

CODA

And I'm lay - ing out __ my win - ter clothes __ and wish - ing I ____ was gone, go - ing home, _ where the New York Cit - y win - ters are - n't bleed - ing me. _____ Lead - ing

me, _____ go - ing home. _

In the clear - ing stands a box - er, and a fight-

- er by his trade, and he car - ries the re - mind - ers of

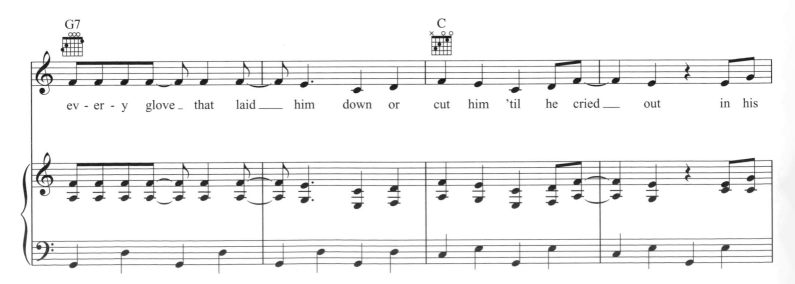

ev - er - y glove _ that laid _ him down or cut him 'til he cried _ out in his

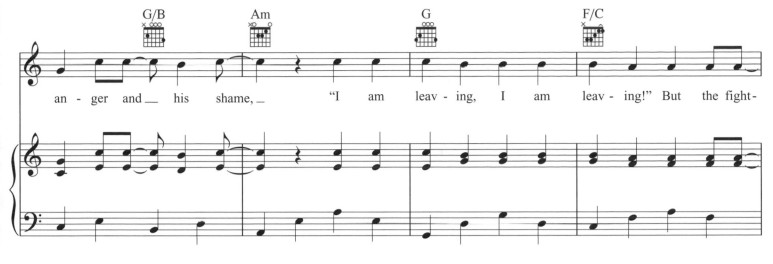

an - ger and __ his shame, __ "I am leav - ing, I am leav - ing!" But the fight-

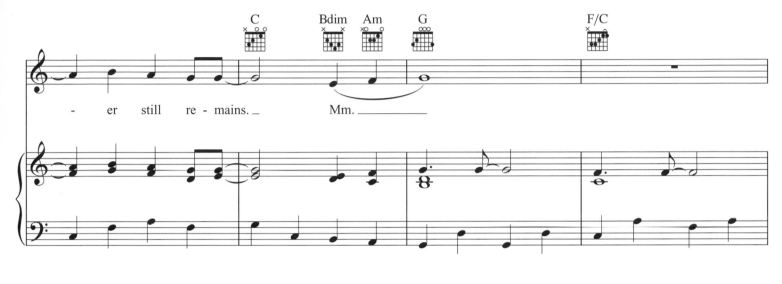

- er still re - mains. __ Mm. _____

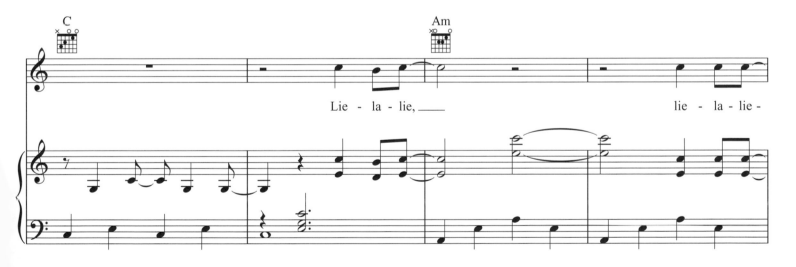

Lie - la - lie, _____ lie - la - lie -

- la - lie - la - lie, _____ lie - la - lie, _____ lie - la - lie -

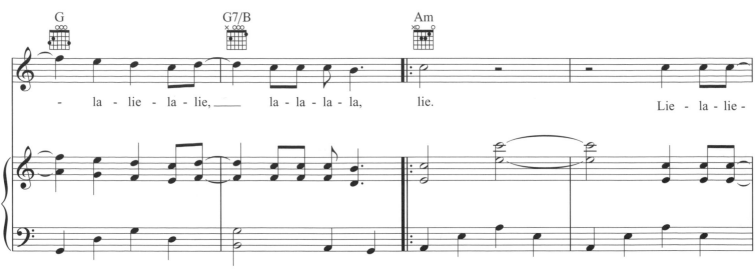

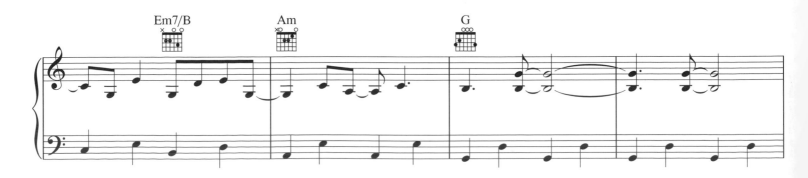

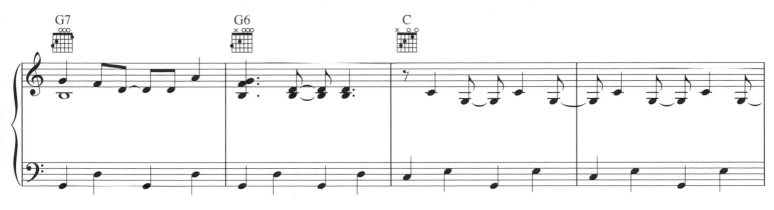

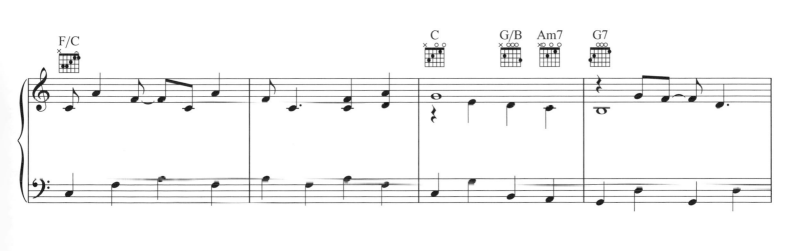

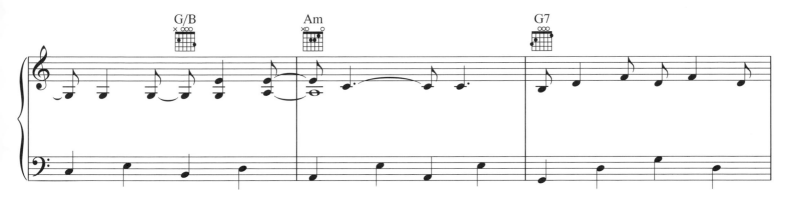

THE END OF THE INNOCENCE

Words and Music by BRUCE HORNSBY
and DON HENLEY

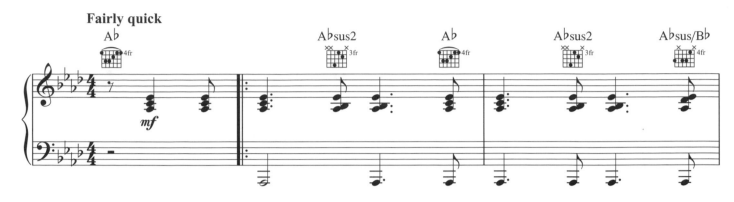

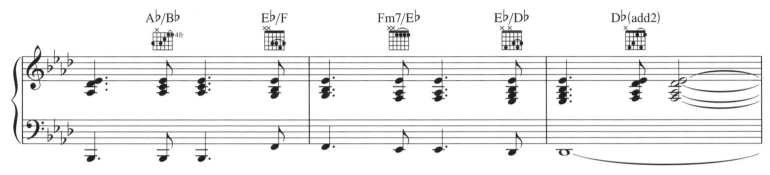

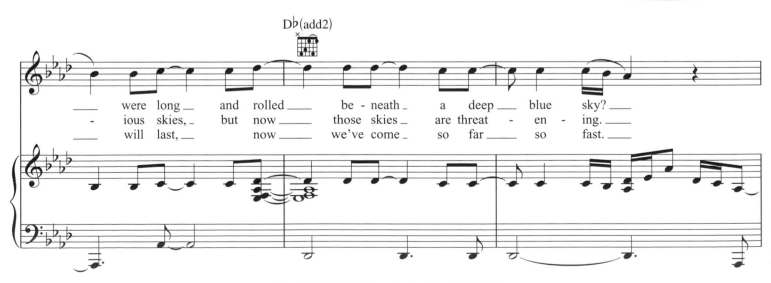

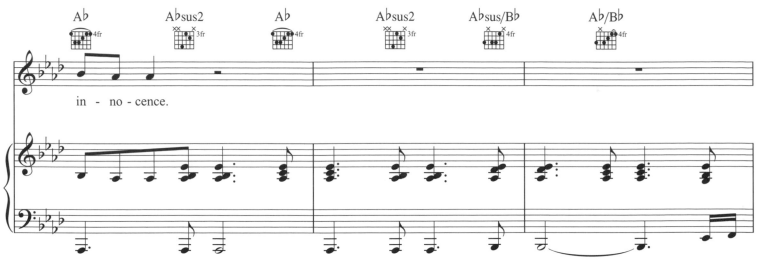

in - no - cence.

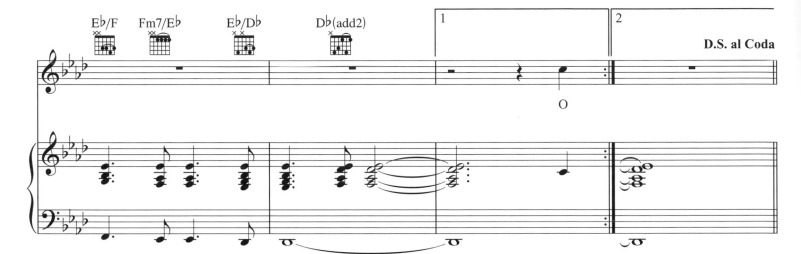

D.S. al Coda

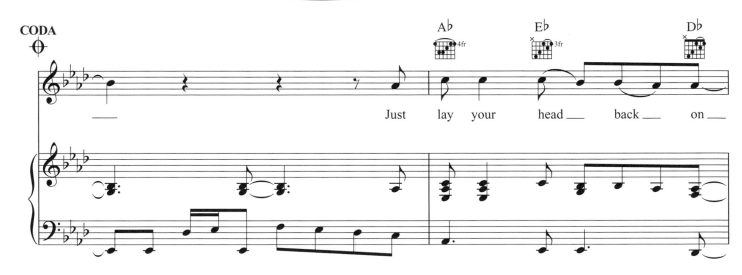

CODA

Just lay your head ___ back ___ on ___

___ the ground ___ and let your hair ___ fall all ___ a - round ___ me. ___

Of-fer up ___ your best ___ de-fense, ___ but this is the end, ___

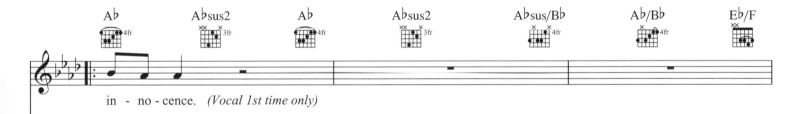

this is the end _____ of the

in - no - cence. *(Vocal 1st time only)*

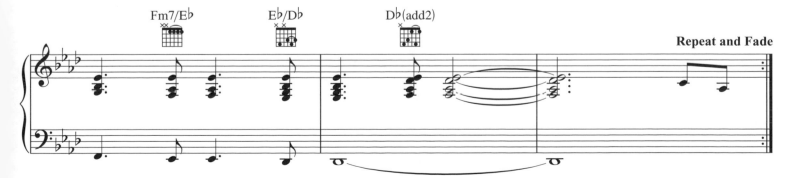

Repeat and Fade

EVE OF DESTRUCTION

Words and Music by P.F. SLOAN
and STEVE BARRI

1. The East-ern world _ it is ex-plod-in',
3. *(See additional lyrics)*

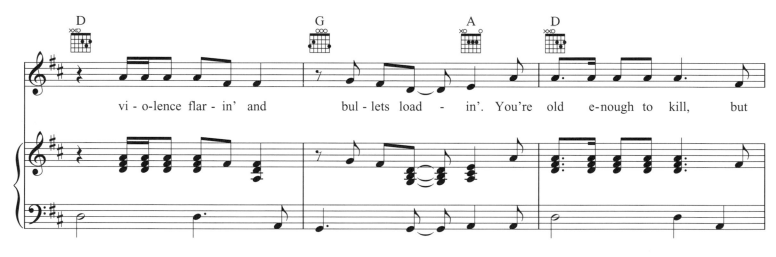

vi-o-lence flar-in' and bul-lets load - in'. You're old e-nough to kill, but

not for _ vot-in'. You don't be-lieve in war, but what's that gun you're tot - in'? And

Chorus

even the Jor-dan Riv-er has bod-ies float-in'! But you tell me

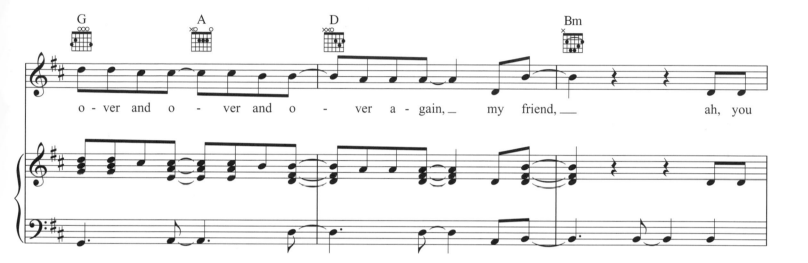

o-ver and o-ver and o-ver a-gain,___ my friend,___ ah, you

don't be-lieve we're on the eve___ of de-struc-tion._____

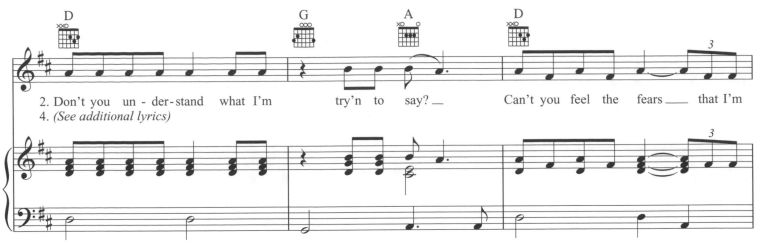

2. Don't you un-der-stand what I'm try'n to say? ___ Can't you feel the fears ___ that I'm
4. *(See additional lyrics)*

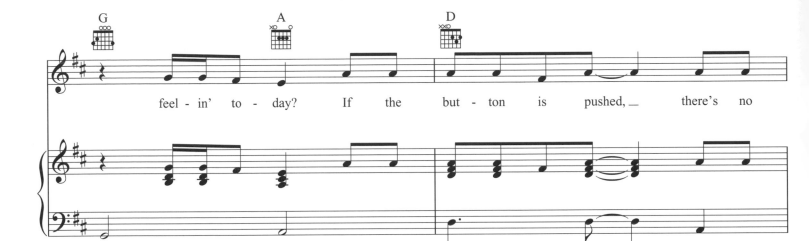

feel-in' to-day? If the but-ton is pushed, ___ there's no

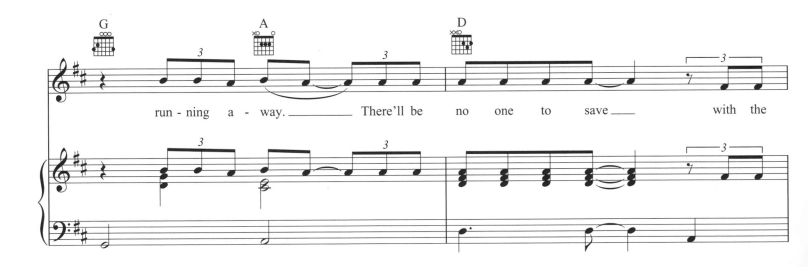

run-ning a-way. _____ There'll be no one to save ___ with the

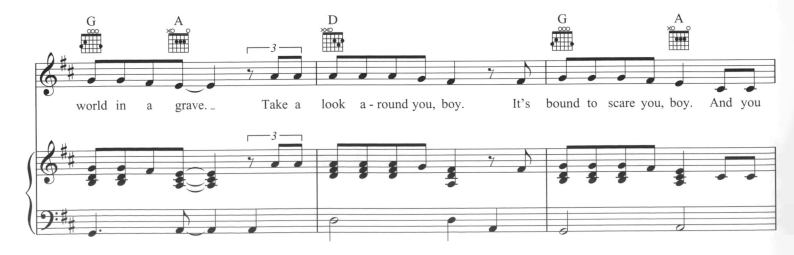

world in a grave. ___ Take a look a-round you, boy. It's bound to scare you, boy. And you

Chorus

tell me o - ver and o - ver and o - ver a - gain, __ my friend, __

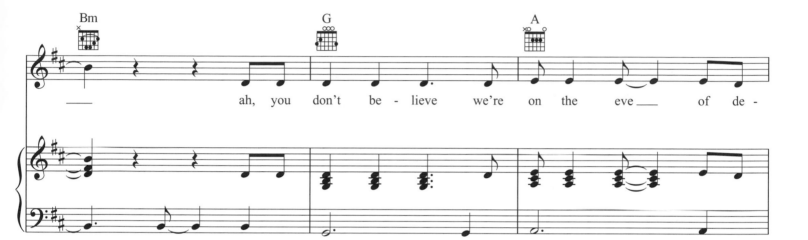

__ ah, you don't be - lieve we're on the eve __ of de -

struc - tion. _____

Yeah, my

You don't be-lieve we're on the eve___ of de-struc-tion.___

Additional Lyrics

3. Yeah, my blood's so mad, feels like coagulatin'
   I'm sittin' here just contemplatin'
   You can't twist the truth, it knows no regulatin'
   And a handful of Senators don't pass legislation
   Marches alone can't bring integration
   When human respect is disintegratin'
   This whole crazy world is just too frustratin'. But you...
   Chorus

4. Think of all the hate there is in Red China
   Then take a look around to Selma, Alabama!
   You may leave here for four days in space
   But when you return, it's the same old place,
   The pounding drums, the pride and disgrace
   You can bury your dead, but don't leave a trace
   Hate your next-door neighbor, but don't forget to say grace. And you...
   Chorus

FORTUNATE SON

Words and Music by
JOHN FOGERTY

Some folks are born ___ made ___ to wave the flag.
Some folks are born ___ sil - ver spoon in hand.

Ooh, they're red, white and blue. ___
Lord, don't they help them-selves, ___

___ now. ___
___ now. ___

And when ___ the band ___ plays "Hail ___ To The Chief,"
And when ___ the tax ___ man comes ___ to the door,

*Recorded a half step lower.
**Vocal sung as written.

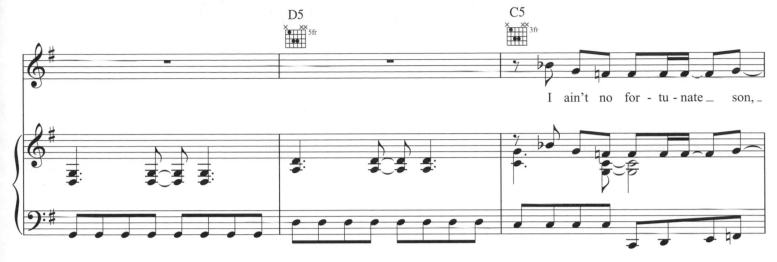

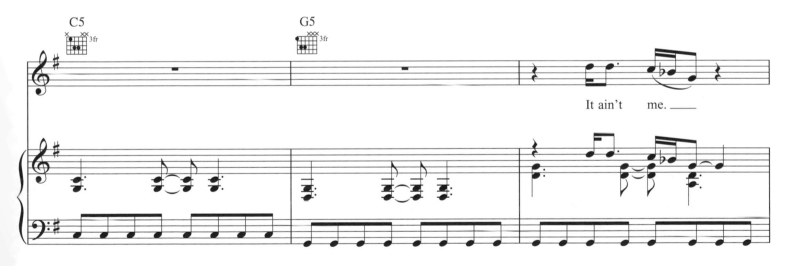

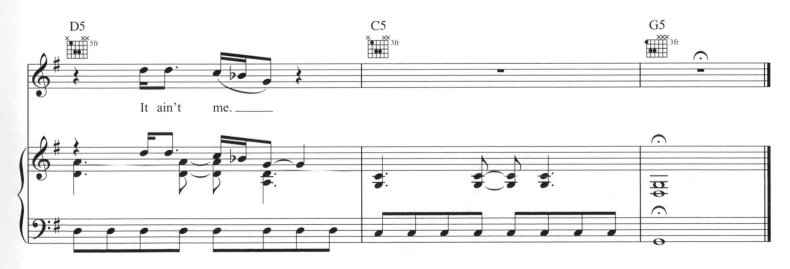

FOR WHAT IT'S WORTH

Words and Music by
STEPHEN STILLS

Slow Rock beat

There's some-thing hap-pen-ing here. What it is ain't ex-act-ly clear. There's a man with a gun o-ver there

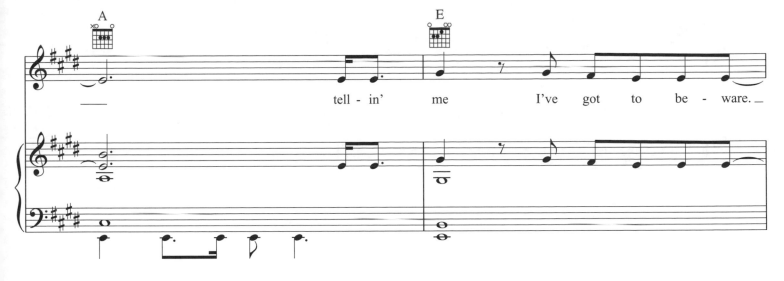

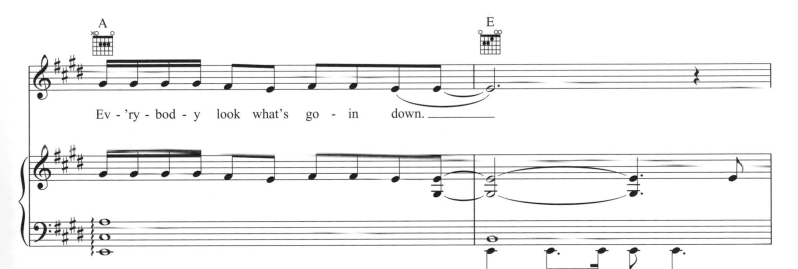

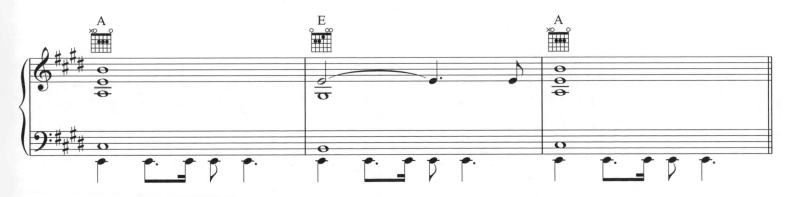

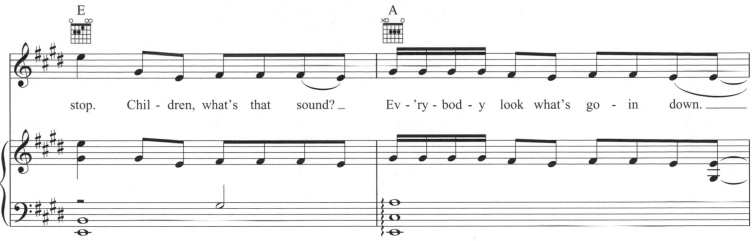

stop. Chil - dren, what's that sound? _ Ev - 'ry - bod - y look what's go - in down. _____

D.S. al Coda

CODA

take you a - way. _ You bet - ter

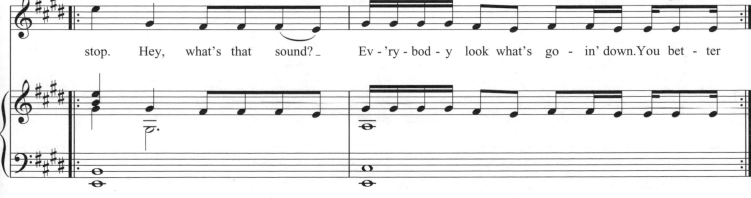

Repeat and Fade

stop. Hey, what's that sound? _ Ev - 'ry - bod - y look what's go - in' down. You bet - ter

GET UP STAND UP

Words and Music by BOB MARLEY
and PETER TOSH

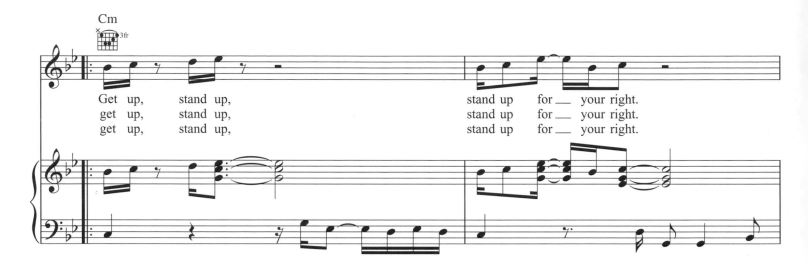

that glit-ters is gold? ___ And half ___ the sto-ry has nev-er been told. ___ So
if you know what life is worth, you ___ would look for yours on earth. ___ And
some peo - ple some-times, but you can't fool all the peo - ple all the time. ___ So

1, 2

now you see ___ the light, aay. ___ Stand up for ___ your right. ___ Come on,
now you see ___ the light. You ___ stand up for ___ your right. ___ Yah, _
now we see ___ the light. We gon-na

3

stand up for ___ our right. So ___ you'd bet - ter get up, } stand up,
Get up, }

Repeat and Fade

stand up for ___ your right. Get up, stand up, don't give up ___ the fight.

GIVE PEACE A CHANCE

Words and Music by
JOHN LENNON

Is - n't it the most?
Bye - bye Bye- byes.
Con - grat - u - la - tions.
Al - len Gins- berg, Ha - re Krish - na Ha - re, Ha - re Krish - na,

All we ___ are

say - ing ___ is give peace ___ a

chance. ___ All we ___ are

say - ing ___ is give peace ___ a

chance. _____ C'- mon.

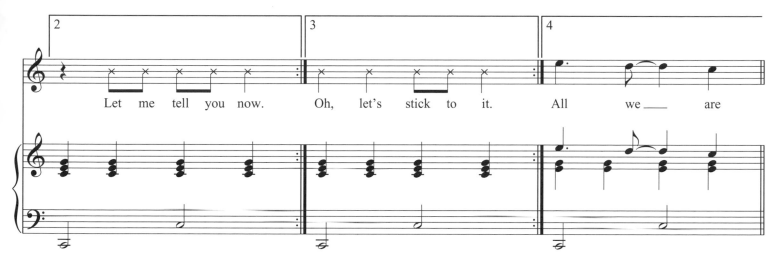

Let me tell you now. Oh, let's stick to it. All we ___ are

say - ing _____ is give peace a

Repeat ad lib. and Fade

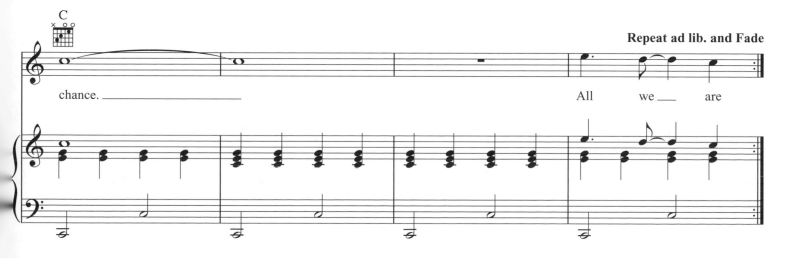

chance. _____ All we ___ are

HURRICANE

Words and Music by BOB DYLAN
and JACQUES LEVY

Moderately

1. Pis - tol shots ring out in a bar - room night. __ En - ter Pat - ty Val - en - tine from the
2.–11. (See additional lyrics)
(D.S.) Instrumental and fade

up - per hall. __ She sees a bar - tend - er ly - in' in a pool of blood. __

Cries out, "My God, they killed __ them all!" ____ Here comes the sto - ry of the Hur - ri - cane, __

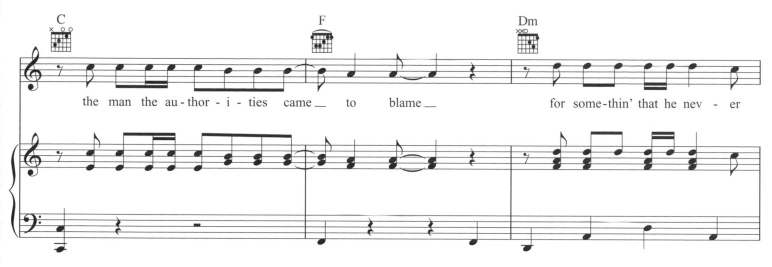

the man the au-thor-i-ties came to blame for some-thin' that he nev - er

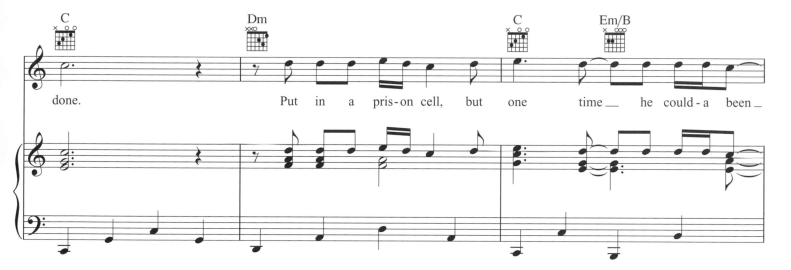

done. Put in a pris-on cell, but one time he could-a been

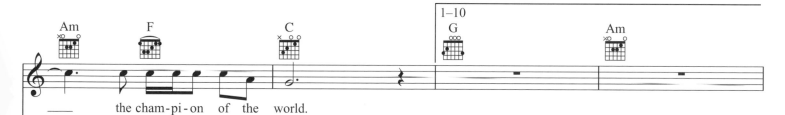

the cham-pi-on of the world.

D.S. and Fade

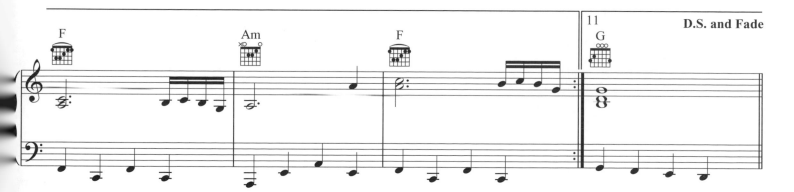

Additional Lyrics

2. Three bodies lying there does Patty see
   And another man named Bello movin' around mysteriously.
   "I didn't do it," he says, and he holds up his hands,
   "I was only robbing the register. I hope you understand.
   I saw 'em leavin,' he says, and he stops,
   "One of us had better hurry and call the cops."
   And so Patty calls the cops
   And they arrive on the scene with their red lights flashin'
   In the hot New Jersey night.

3. Meanwhile, far away in another part of town,
   Rubin Carter and some friends are drivin' around.
   The number one contender for the middleweight crown
   Had no idea what kinda shit was about to go down.
   When the cop pulled him over to the side of the road
   Just like the time before and the time before that,
   In Patterson that's just the way things go.
   If you're black, you might as well not show up on the street
   'Less you wanna draw the heat.

4. Alfred Bello had a partner and he had a rap for the cops.
   Him and Arthur Dexter Bradley were just out prowlin' around.
   He said, "I saw two men runnin' out, they looked
     like middleweights.
   They jumped into a white car with out-of-state plates."
   And Miss Patty Valentine just nodded her head.
   Cop said, "Wait a minute, boys. This one's not dead."
   So they took him to the infirmary,
   And though this man could hardly see,
   They told him that he could identify the guilty men.

5. Four hours later and they haul Rubin in,
   Bring him to the hospital and take him upstairs.
   The wounded man looks up through his one dyin' eye,
   Says, "Wha'd you bring him in here for? He ain't the guy!"
   Here's the story of the Hurricane,
   The man the authorities came to blame
   For somethin' that he never done.
   Put in a prison cell, but one time he could-a been
   The champion of the world.

6. Four months later, the ghettoes are in flame.
   Rubin's in South America, fightin' for his name,
   While Arthur Dexter Bradley's still in the robbery game.
   And the cops are puttin' the screws to him, lookin' for
     somebody to blame,
   "Remember that murder that happened in a bar?"
   "Remember you said you saw the getaway car?"
   "You think you'd like to play ball with the law?"
   "Think it mighta been that fighter that you saw
     runnin' that night?"
   "Don't forget that you are white."

7. Arthur Dexter Bradley said, "I'm really not sure."
   Cops said, "A poor boy like you could use a break.
   We got you for the motel job and we're talkin' to
     your friend Bello.
   Now you don't wanna have to go back to jail, be a nice fellow.
   You'll be doin' society a favor,
   That sonofabitch is brave and gettin' braver.
   We want to put his ass in stir.
   We want to pin this triple murder on him,
   He ain't no Gentleman Jim."

8. Rubin could take a man out with just one punch,
   But he never did like to talk about it all that much.
   It's my work, he'd say, and I do it for pay
   And when it's over I'd just as soon go on my way
   Up to some paradise
   Where the trout streams flow and the air is nice
   And ride a horse along a trail.
   But then they took him to the jail house
   Where they try to turn a man into a mouse.

9. All of Rubin's cards were marked in advance.
   The trial was a pig-circus, he never had a chance.
   The judge made Rubin's witnesses drunkards from the slums.
   To the white folks who watched he was a revolutionary bum.
   And to the black folks he was just a crazy nigger,
   No one doubted that he pulled the trigger.
   And though they could not produce the gun,
   The D.A. said he was the one who did the deed,
   And the all-white jury agreed.

10. Rubin Carter was falsely tried.
    The crime was murder "one", guess who testified?
    Bello and Bradley, and they both baldly lied,
    And the newspapers, they all went along for the ride.
    How can the life of such a man
    Be in the palm of some fool's hand?
    To see him obviously framed
    Couldn't help but make me feel ashamed to live in a land
    Where justice is a game.

11. Now all the criminals in their coats and their ties
    Are free to drink martinis and watch the sun rise,
    While Rubin sits like Buddha in a ten-foot cell,
    An innocent man in a living hell.
    That's the story of the Hurricane,
    But it won't be over till they clear his name
    And give him back the time he's done.
    Put in a prison cell, but one time he coulda been
    The champion of the world.

MASTERS OF WAR

Words and Music by
BOB DYLAN

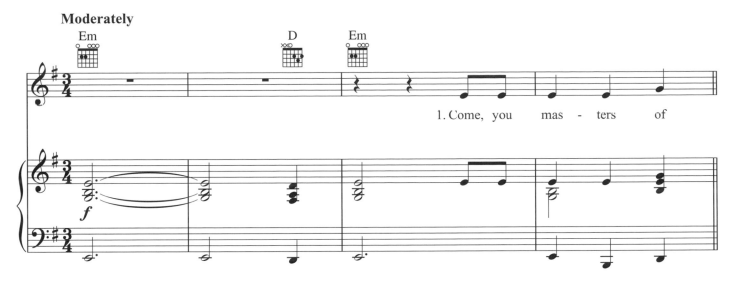

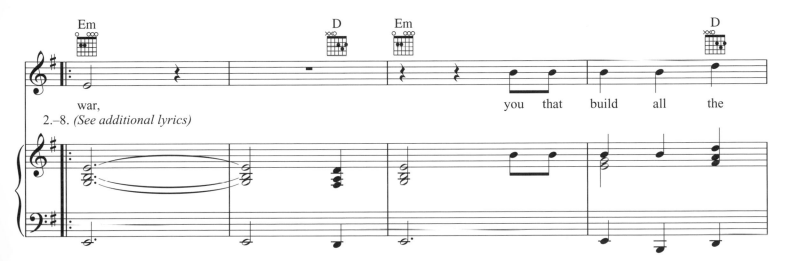

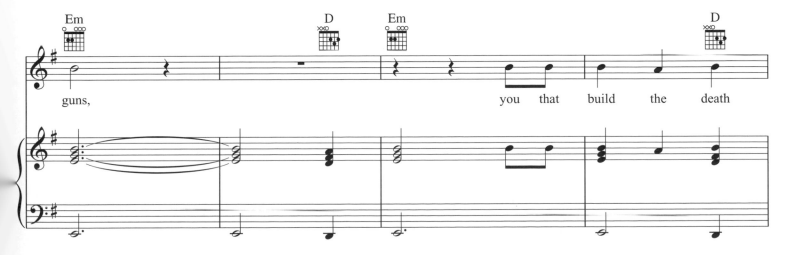

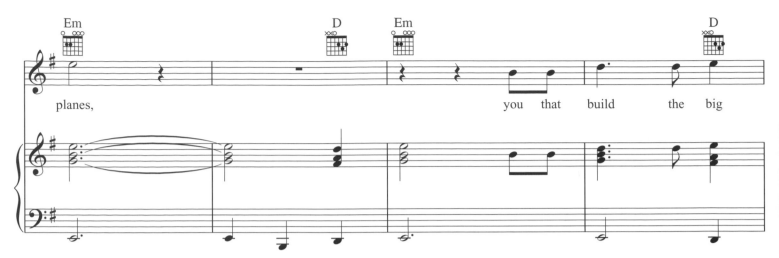

planes,   you that build the big

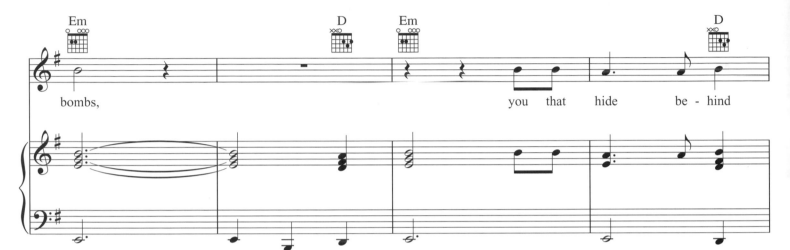

bombs,   you that hide be - hind

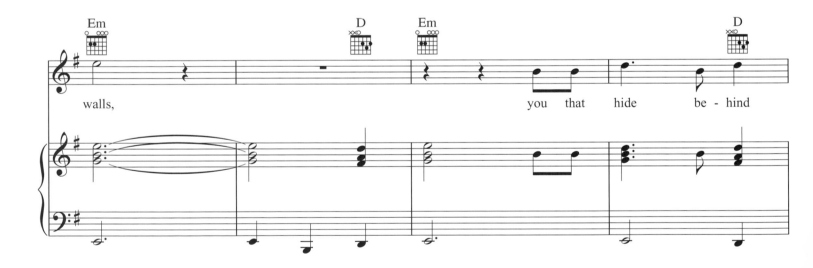

walls,   you that hide be - hind

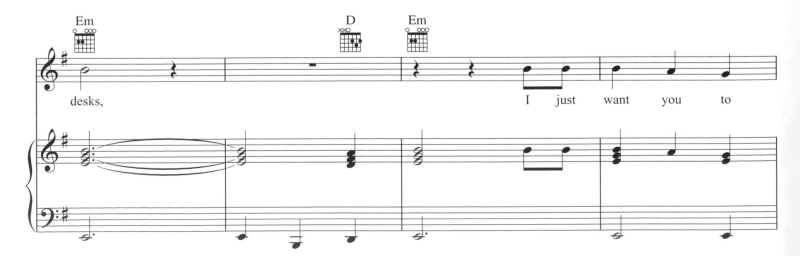

desks,   I just want you to

know   I   can   see   through   your   masks.

1–7
Em

2. You   that   nev - er   done

8
Em

Additional Lyrics

2. You that never done nothin'
   But build to destroy
   You play with my world
   Like it's your little toy
   You put a gun in my hand
   And you hide from my eyes
   And you turn and run farther
   When the fast bullets fly.

3. Like Judas of old
   You lie and deceive
   A world war can be won
   You want me to believe
   But I see through your eyes
   And I see through your brain
   Like I see through the water
   That runs down my drain.

4. You fasten all the triggers
   For the others to fire
   And you sit back and watch
   And the death count gets higher
   You hide in your mansion'
   As young people's blood
   Flows out of their bodies
   And is buried in the mud.

5. You've thrown the worst fear
   That can ever be hurled
   Fear to bring children
   Into the world
   For threatening my baby
   Unborn and unnamed
   You ain't worth the blood
   That runs in your veins.

6. How much do I know
   To talk out of turn
   You might say that I'm young
   You might say I'm unlearned
   But there's one thing I know
   Though I'm younger than you
   That even Jesus would never
   Forgive what you do.

7. Let me ask you one question:
   Is your money that good?
   Will it buy you forgiveness?
   Do you think that it could?
   I think you will find
   When your death takes its toll,
   All the money you made
   Will never buy back your soul.

8. And I hope that you die
   And your death'll come soon
   I will follow your casket
   In the pale afternoon
   And I'll watch while you're lowered
   Down to your deathbed
   And I'll stand over your grave
   'Til I'm sure that you're dead.

I FEEL LIKE I'M FIXIN' TO DIE RAG

Words and Music by
JOE McDONALD

Medium, in 2

one, two, three, what are we fight-ing for? Don't ask me, I

don't give a damn, next stop is Vi-et-nam. And it's five, six,

sev-en, o-pen up the pearl-y gates; There ain't no time to

won-der why. Whoop-ee, _____ we're all gon-na die! die!

I WANT TO BREAK FREE

Words and Music by
JOHN DEACON

Moderately

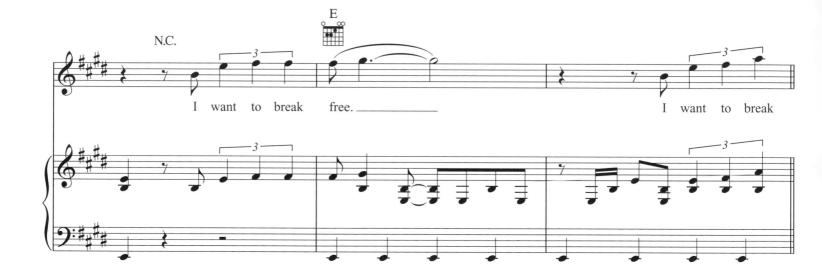

I want to break free. _____ I want to break

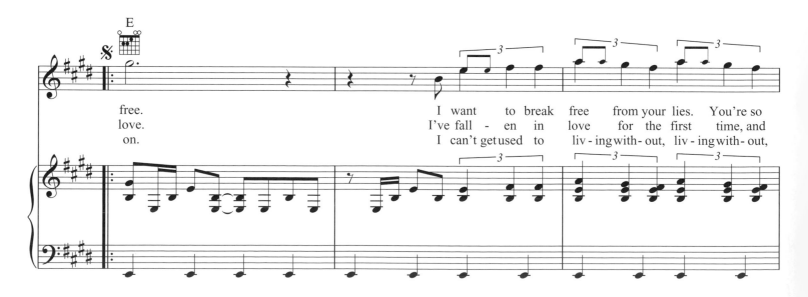

free.
love.
on.

I want to break free from your lies. You're so
I've fall-en in love for the first time, and
I can't get used to liv-ing with-out, liv-ing with-out,

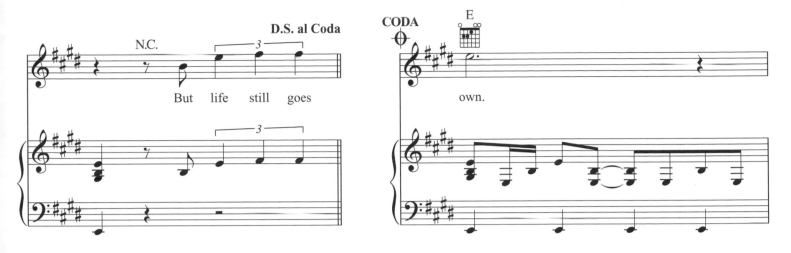

IMAGINE

Words and Music by
JOHN LENNON

I-mag-ine there's no heav-en. ___

It's eas-y if you ___ try. ___ No hell ___ be-low us, ___

___ a-bove us on-ly sky. ___

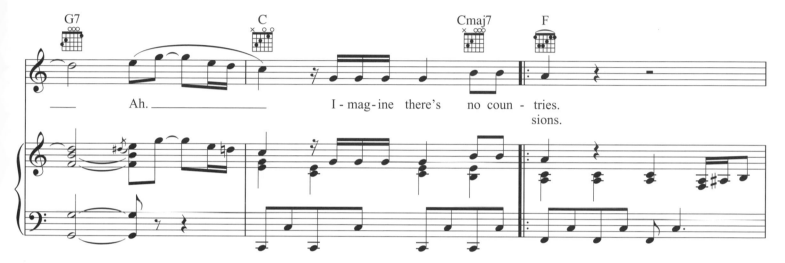

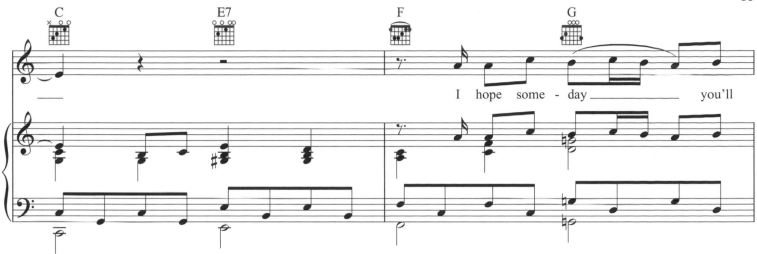

I hope some-day _____ you'll

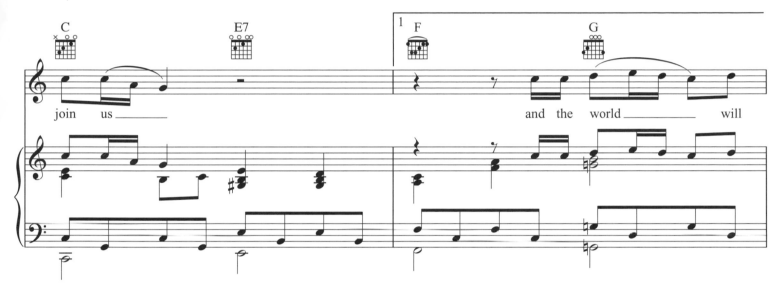

join us _____ and the world _____ will

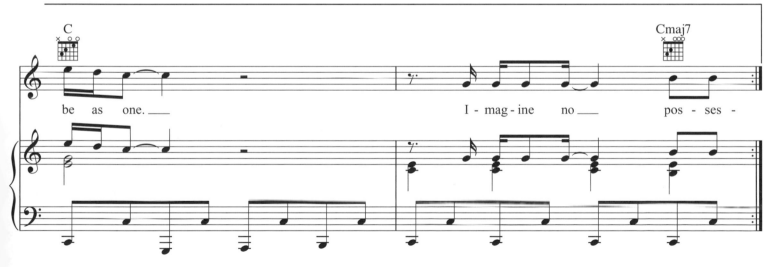

be as one. ____ I - mag - ine no ___ pos - ses -

and the world _____ will live as one. ____

PEACE TRAIN

Words and Music by
CAT STEVENS

Moderately, in 2

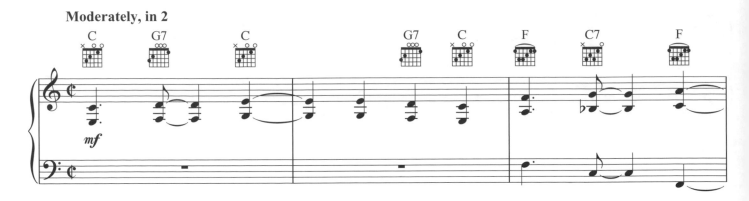

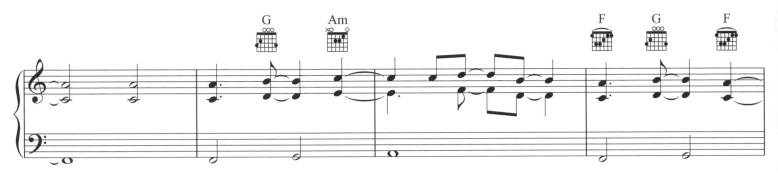

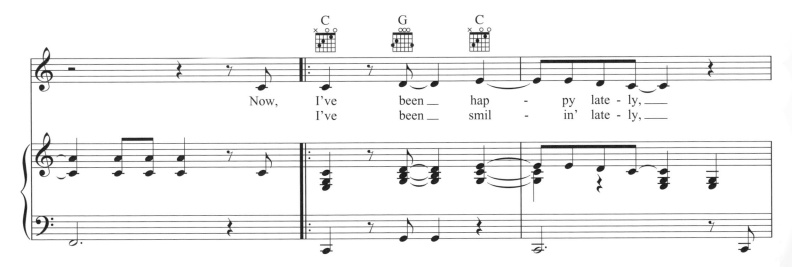

Now,   I've   been ___ hap - py late - ly, ___
I've   been ___ smil - in' late - ly, ___

think - in' a - bout   the good things ___ to come,   and   I ___ be - lieve
dream - in' a - bout   the world ___ as one,   and   I ___ be - lieve

it could __ be. __ Some-thing good has _____ be - gun. Oh,
it could __ be. __ Some - day it's goin' _____ to come. 'Cause

out on __ the edge ____ of dark - ness __ there rides __ a peace

train. Oh, peace train, __ take _____ this coun - try,

come take __ me home _____ a - gain. Now, I've been __ smil -

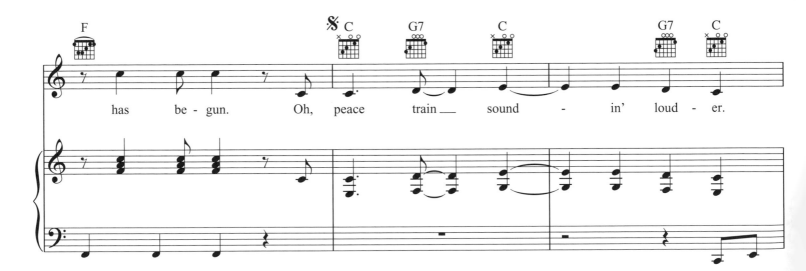

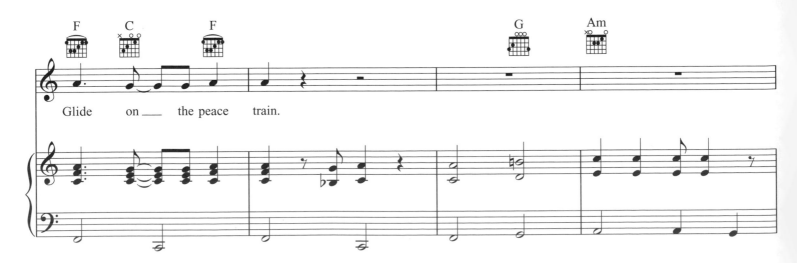

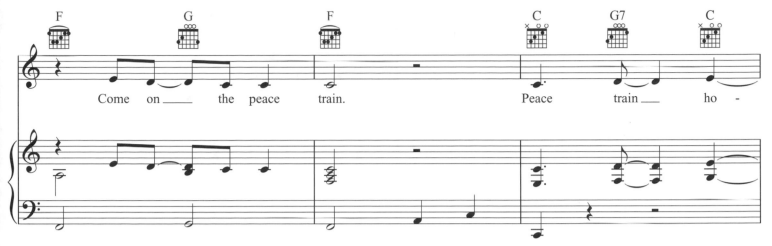

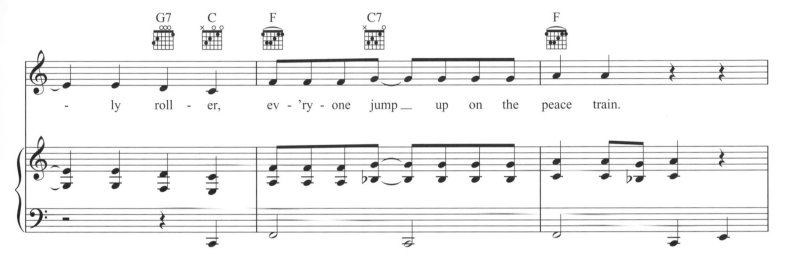

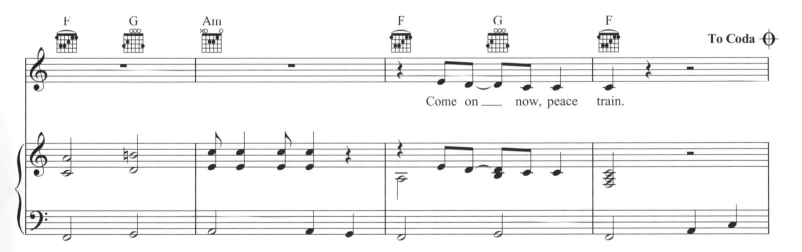

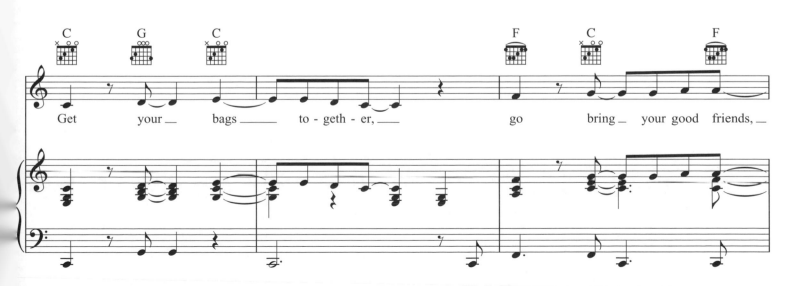

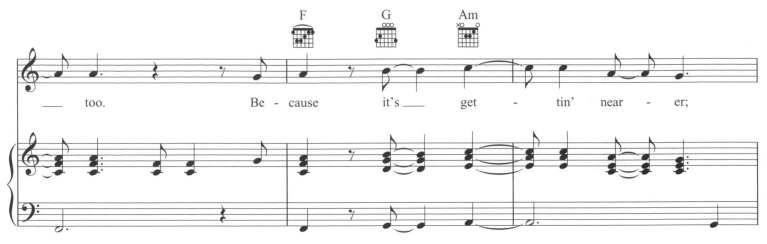

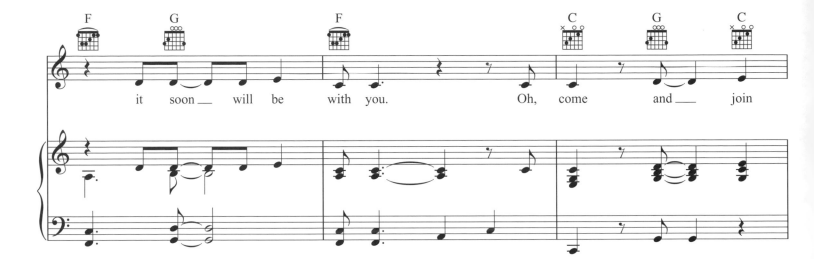

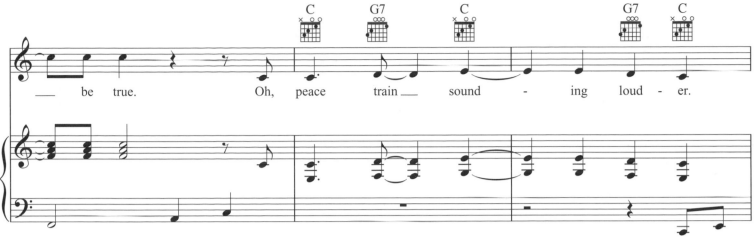

be true. Oh, peace train _____ sound - ing loud - er.

Glide on _____ the peace train. Ooh. _____

_____ Come on _____ now, peace train, peace train.

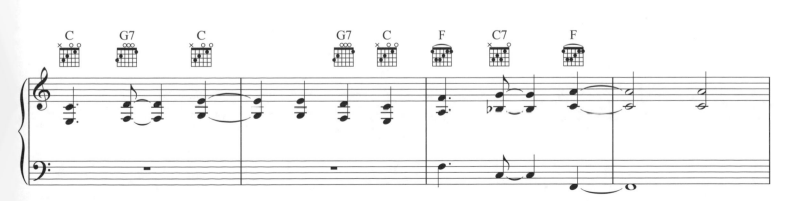

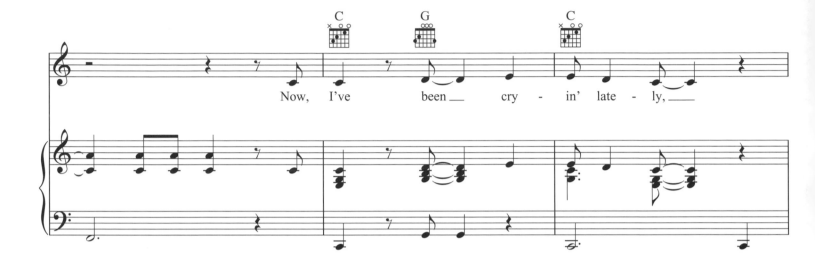

Now, I've been ___ cry - in' late - ly, ___

think-in' a-bout the world as it is. Why must ___ we go ___

___ on hat - ing? Why can't ___ we live in bliss? 'Cause

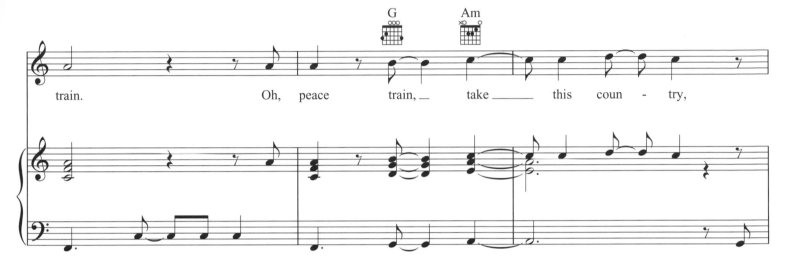

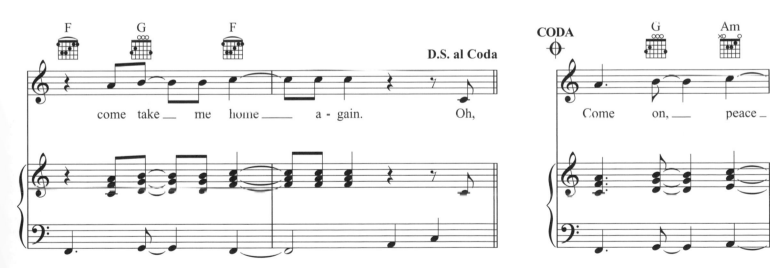

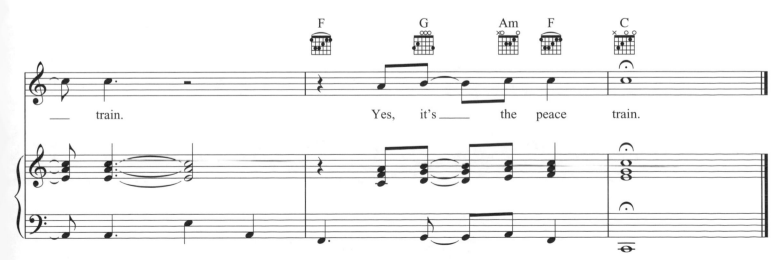

POWER TO THE PEOPLE

Words and Music by
JOHN LENNON

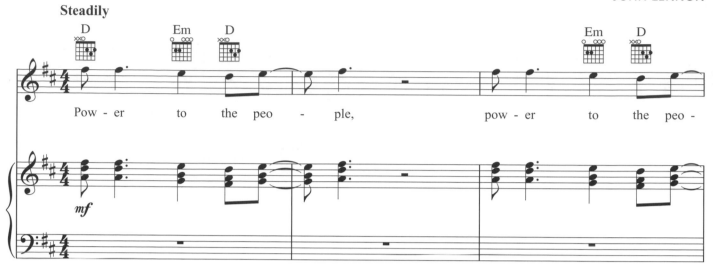

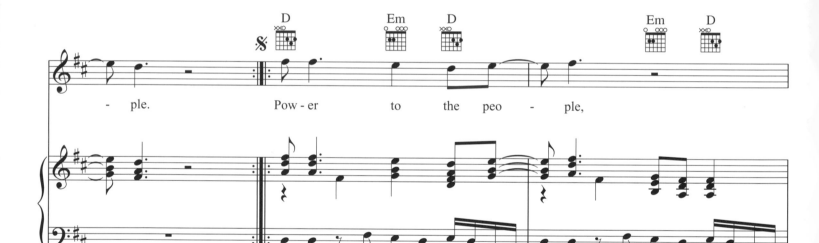

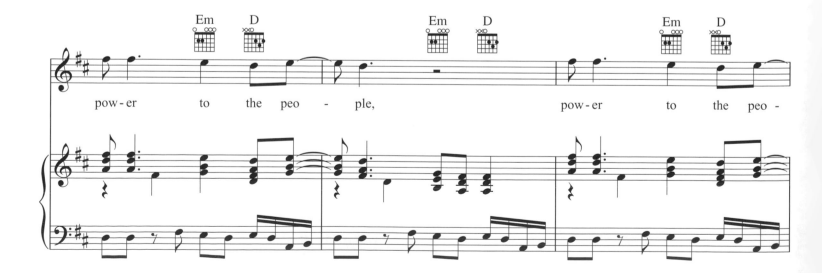

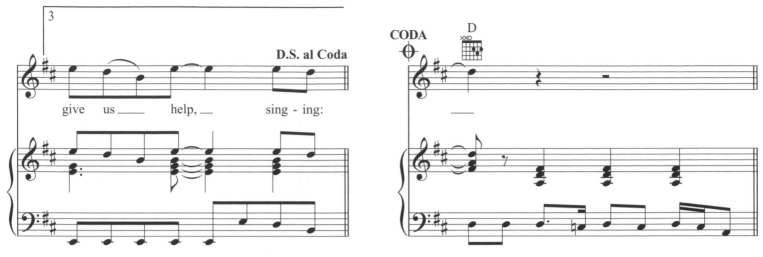

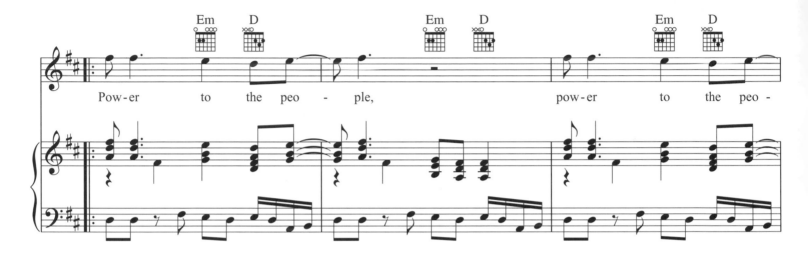

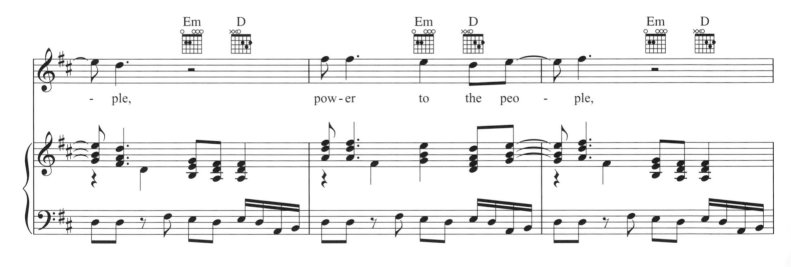

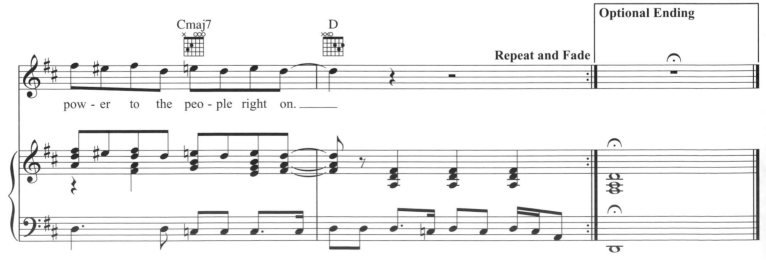

PEOPLE GOT TO BE FREE

Words and Music by FELIX CAVALIERE
and EDWARD BRIGATI, JR.

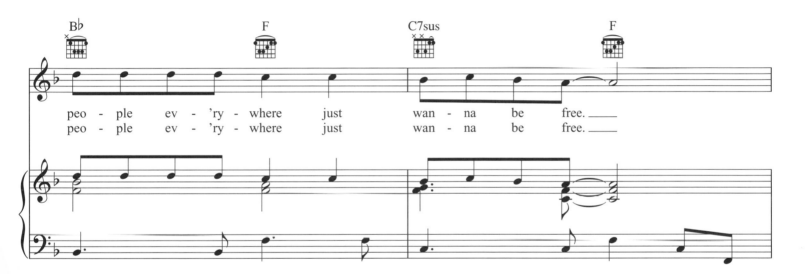

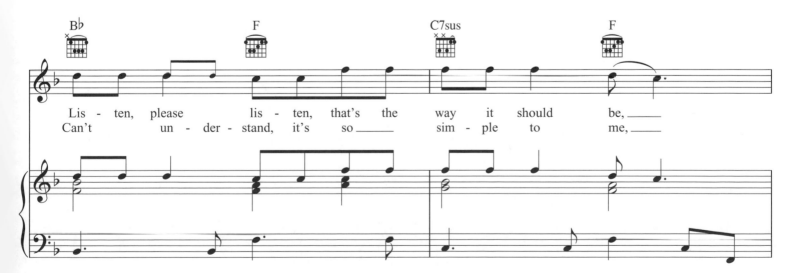

peace in the val - ley, peo - ple got to be free. _____
peo - ple ev - 'ry - where _ just _ got to be free. _____

You should see _____ what a love - ly, love - ly world this would be _____
If there's a man _____ who is down and needs a help - ing hand, _

_____ if ev - er - y - one _____ learned to live to - geth -
_____ all it takes is you to un - der - stand _____ and to pull him through. _

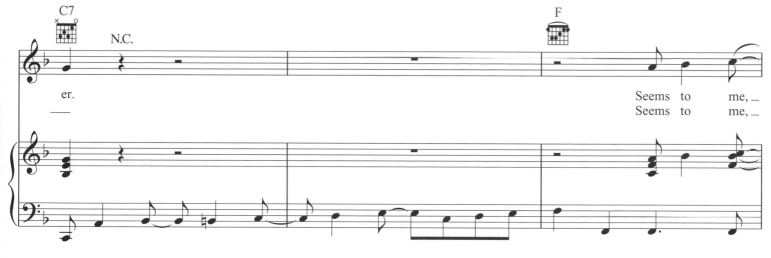

er.

Seems to me, __
Seems to me, __

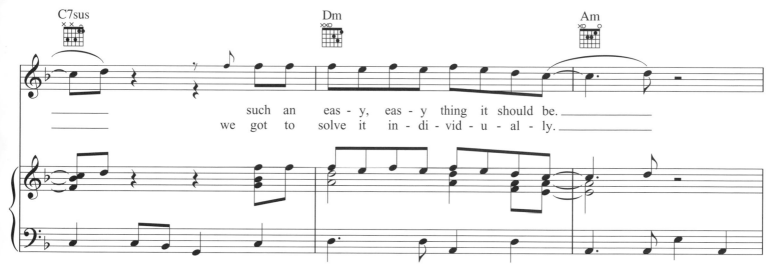

__
__

such an eas-y, eas-y thing it should be. _____
we got to solve it in-di-vid-u-al-ly. _____

Why can't you and me ___ learn to love one an-oth-er?
And I'll do un-to you ___ what you do ___ to

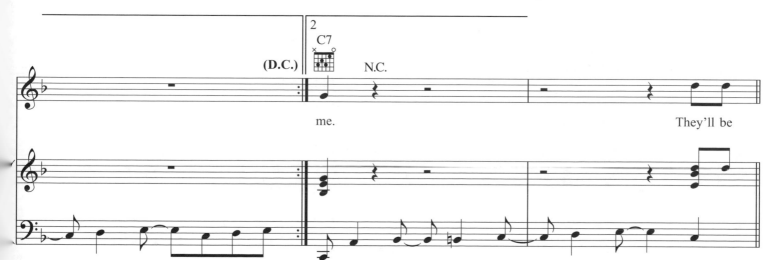

me.

They'll be

shout - in' from the moun - tain on out to the sea, ___ It's e -
Oh, ___ what a feel - in' just come o - ver me. ___

no two ways a - bout it, peo - ple have to be free. ___
nough to move a moun - tain, make a blind ___ man see. ___

Ask me my o - pin - ion, my o - pin - ion will be, ___ it's a
Ev - 'ry - bod - y's danc - in'; come on, let's ___ go see. ___ There's _

nat - 'ral sit - u - a - tion for a man to be free. ___
peace _ in the val - ley, now we all can be free. ___

REVOLUTION

Words and Music by JOHN LENNON
and PAUL McCARTNEY

to change the   world.   You
to see the   plan.   You
to change your   head.   You

tell me that it's ev - o - lu - tion;_____ well,_____ you know,_____
ask me for a con - tri - bu - tion;_____ well,_____ you know,_____
tell me it's the in - sti - tu - tion;_____ well,_____ you know,_____

we all want_____ to change the   world._____
we're all do - ing what we   can._____
you better free_____ your mind in - stead._____

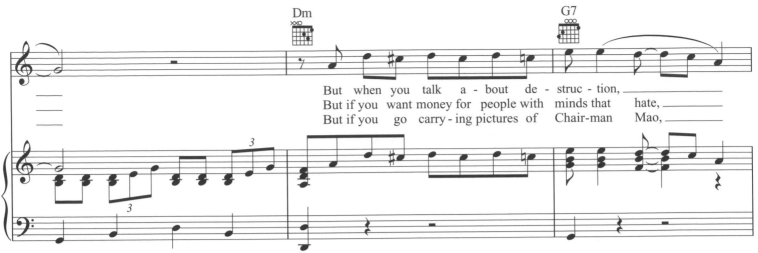

But when you talk a - bout de - struc - tion,
But if you want money for people with minds that hate,
But if you go carry - ing pictures of Chair - man Mao,

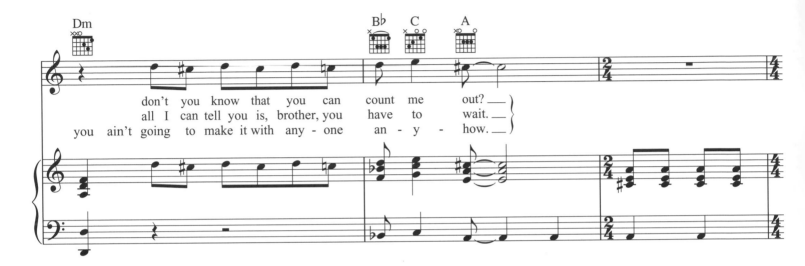

don't you know that you can count me out?
all I can tell you is, brother, you have to wait.
you ain't going to make it with any - one an - y - how.

Don't you know it's gon-na be al - right,

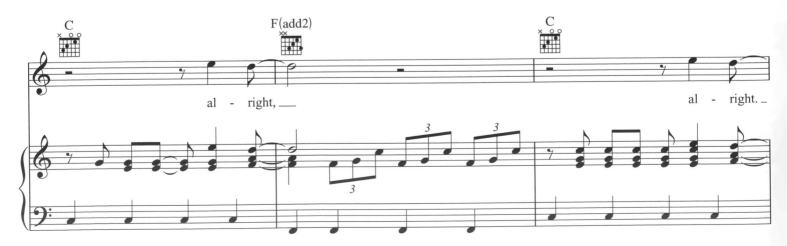

al - right, al - right.

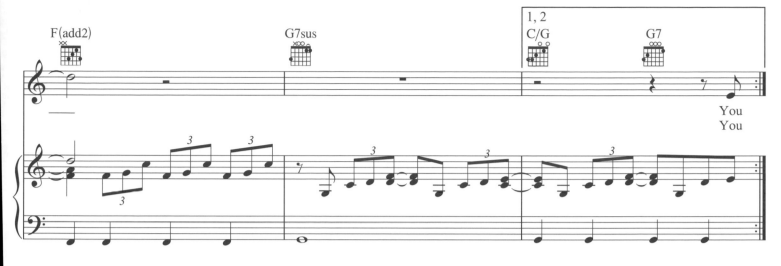

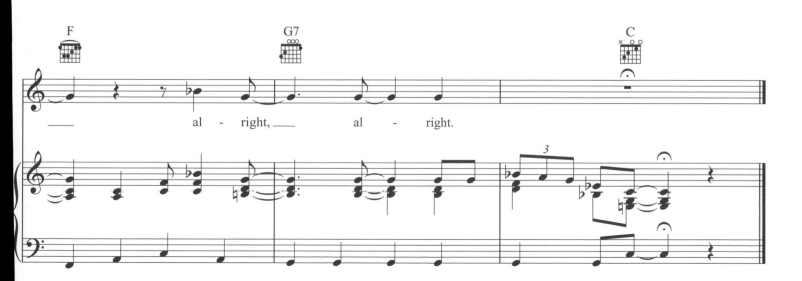

THE REVOLUTION STARTS... NOW

Words and Music by
STEVE EARLE

o - pened up my eyes _____ and I took a look a - round.
work and where you play, _____ where you lay your mon - ey down,
brought what they could bring _____ and no - bod - y went with - out.

To Coda ⊕

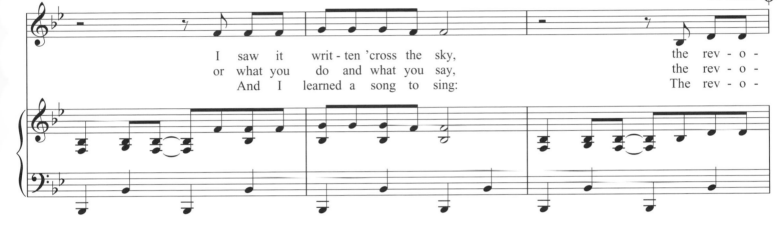

I saw it writ - ten 'cross the sky, the rev - o -
or what you do and what you say, the rev - o -
And I learned a song to sing: The rev - o -

Fm   A♭

lu - tion starts now. }
lu - tion starts now. }   Yeah, the rev - o - lu - tion starts

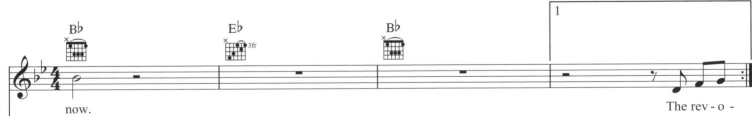

B♭   E♭   B♭   1

now.   The rev - o -

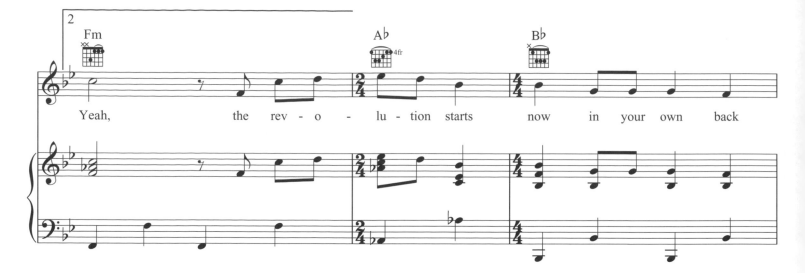

Yeah, the rev - o - lu - tion starts now in your own back

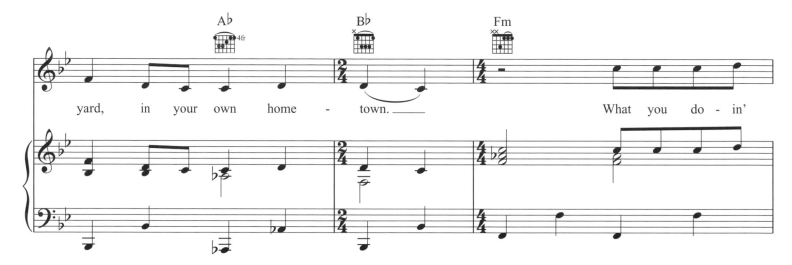

yard, in your own home - town. ____ What you do - in'

stand - in' a - round? __ Just fol - low your heart, __ your rev - o - lu - tion starts

now. *(Vocal 1st time only)*

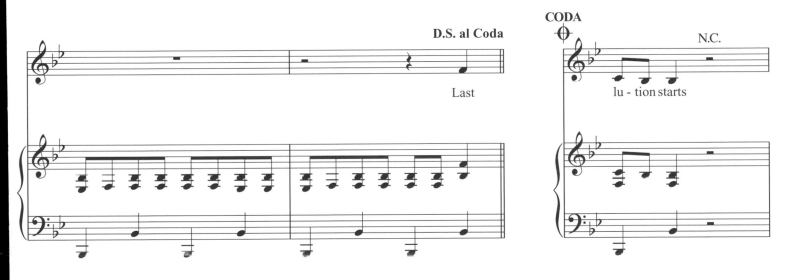

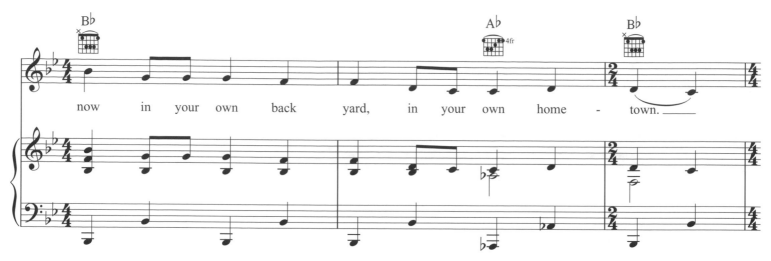

now in your own back yard, in your own home - town. _____

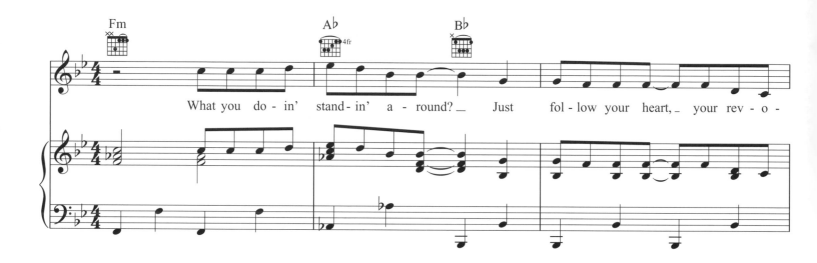

What you do-in' stand-in' a - round? _ Just fol-low your heart, _ your rev-o-

lu - tion starts now. lu - tion starts now.

Optional Ending

Repeat and Fade

ROCK THE CASBAH

Words and Music by JOE STRUMMER,
MICK JONES and TOPPER HEADON

Rock the Cas - bah. Sha - reef _____ don't like it. _____

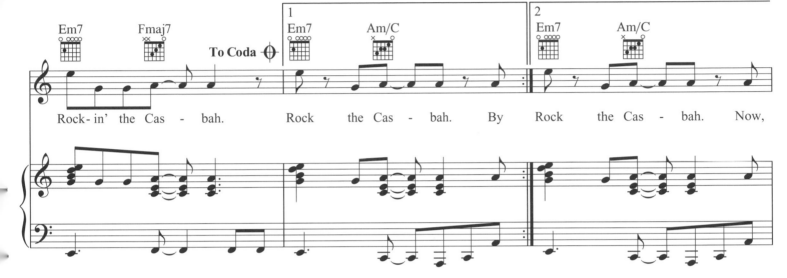

To Coda ⊕ | 1 | 2

Rock-in' the Cas - bah. Rock the Cas - bah. By Rock the Cas - bah. Now,

o - ver at the tem - ple, oh, they real - ly pack 'em in.

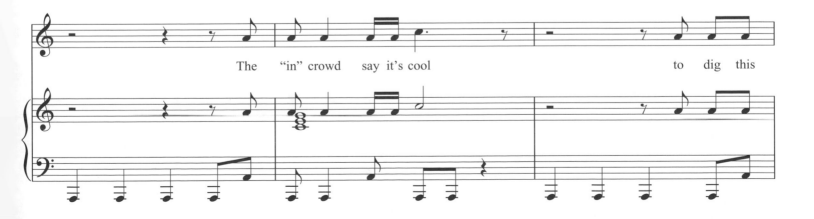

The "in" crowd say it's cool to dig this

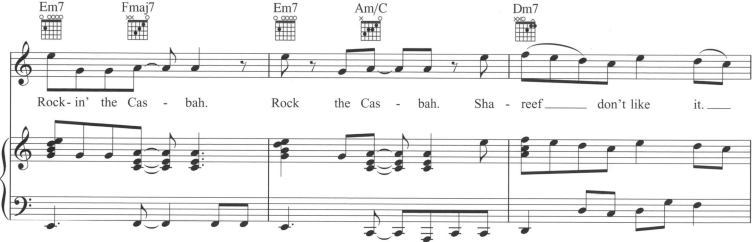

Rock-in' the Cas - bah. Rock the Cas-bah. Sha-reef_____ don't like it.____

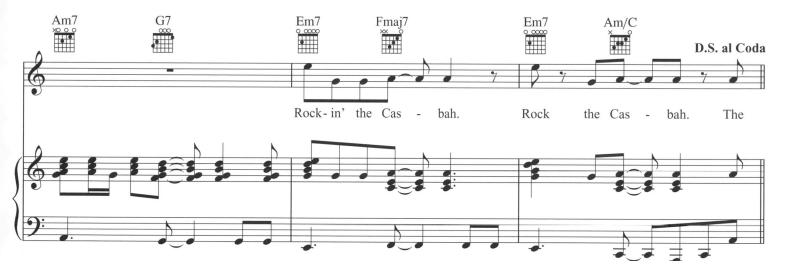

Rock-in' the Cas - bah. Rock the Cas - bah. The

D.S. al Coda

CODA

Rock the Cas - bah. Sha - reef_____ don't like it.____

Repeat and Fade

Rock-in' the Cas - bah. Rock the Cas - bah. Sha-

STRANGE FRUIT

Words and Music by
LEWIS ALLAN

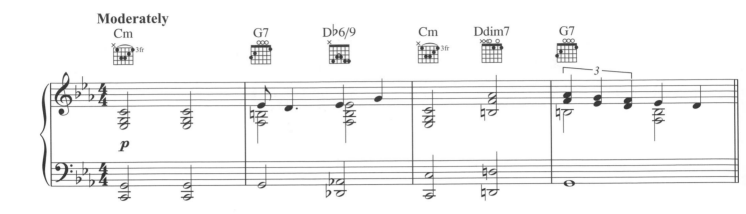

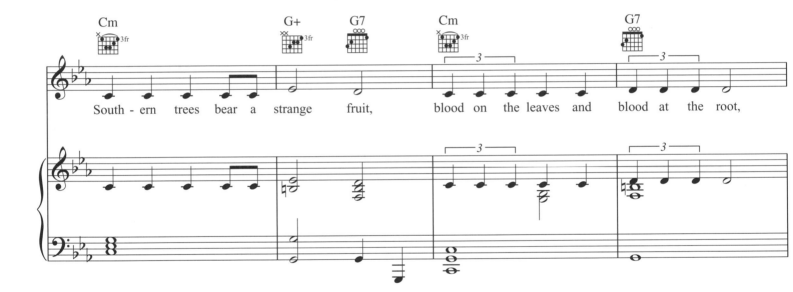

THE TIMES THEY ARE A-CHANGIN'

Words and Music by
BOB DYLAN

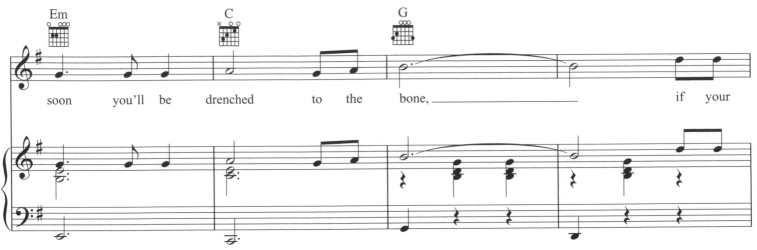

soon you'll be drenched to the bone, _____ if your

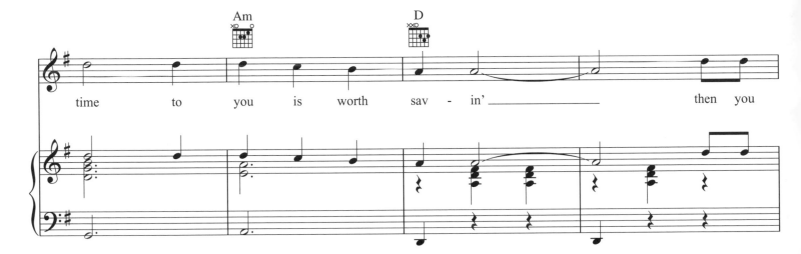

time to you is worth sav - in' _____ then you

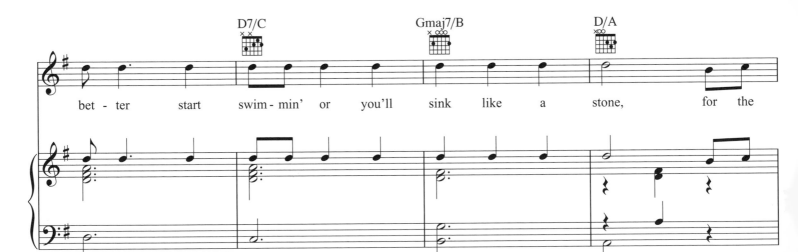

bet - ter start swim - min' or you'll sink like a stone, for the

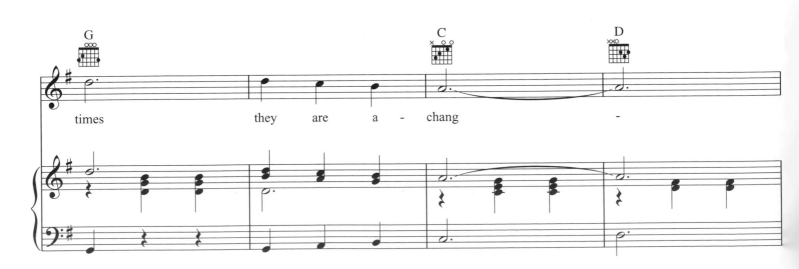

times they are a - chang -

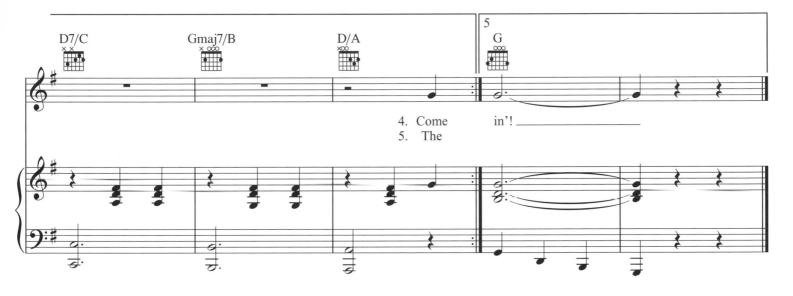

Additional Lyrics

2. Come writers and critics
   Who prophesy with your pen
   And keep your eyes wide
   The chance won't come again.
   And don't speak too soon
   For the wheel's still in spin,
   And there's no tellin' who
   That it's namin'.
   For the loser now
   Will be later to win
   For the times they are a-changin'!

3. Come senators, congressmen
   Please heed the call
   Don't stand in the doorway
   Don't block up the hall.
   For he that gets hurt
   Will be he who has stalled,
   There's a battle
   Outside and it's ragin'.
   It'll soon shake your windows
   And rattle your walls
   For the times they are a-changin'!

4. Come mothers and fathers
   Throughout the land
   And don't criticize
   What you can't understand.
   Your sons and your daughters
   Are beyond your command,
   Your old road is
   Rapidly agin'.
   Please get out of the new one
   If you can't lend your hand
   For the times they are a-changin'!

5. The line it is drawn
   The curse it is cast
   The slow one now will
   Later be fast.
   As the present now
   Will later be past,
   The order is rapidly fadin'.
   And the first one now
   Will later be last
   For the times they are a-changin'!

SUNDAY BLOODY SUNDAY

Words and Music by U2

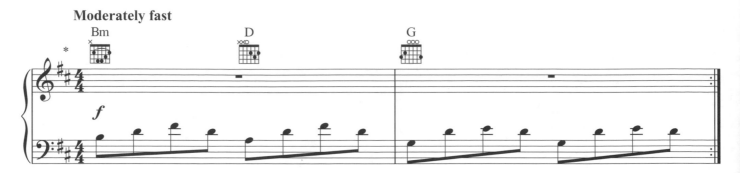

I can't be - lieve _ the news _ to - day. _

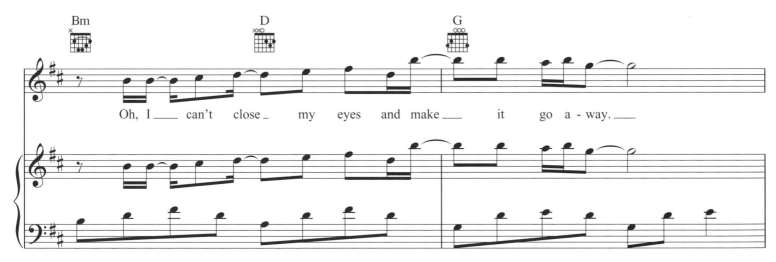

Oh, I _ can't close _ my eyes and make _ it go a - way. _

How long, _____ how long must we sing this song? How long, _____ how

Recorded a half step lower.

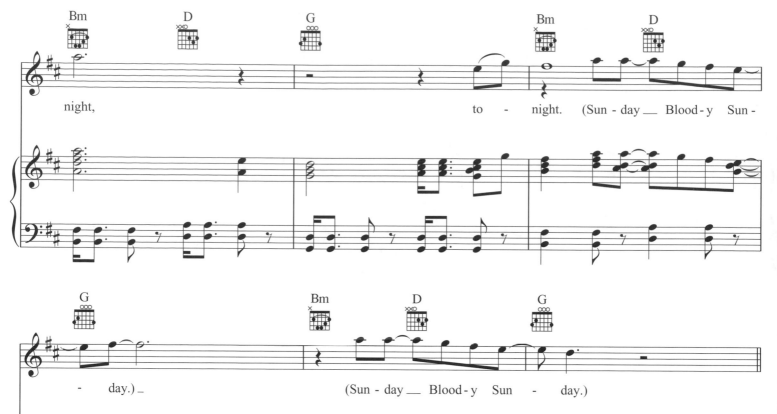

night,   to - night. (Sun - day __ Blood - y Sun -

- day.) __   (Sun - day __ Blood - y Sun - day.)

Play 4 times

Instrumental solo ad lib.

Wipe __ the tears from __ your eyes.   Wipe __ your tears __

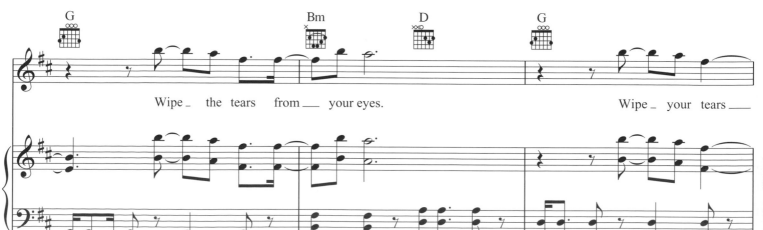

mor - row they _ die. _____ The real bat - tle is _ be - gun _

_ to claim the vic - t'ry Je - sus won _ for

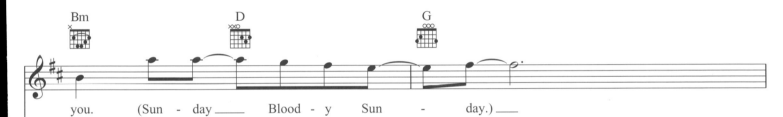

you. (Sun - day ___ Blood - y Sun - day.) ___

(Sun - day ___ Blood - y Sun - day.) _

WAR

Words and Music by NORMAN WHITFIELD
and BARRETT STRONG

Slow Rock, with double-time feel

1. War, uh! What is it good for? Ab-so-lute-ly noth-ing. War, uh! What is it good for? Ab-so-lute-ly
2.–5. *(See additional lyrics)*

War means tears — in thou - sands of moth - ers' eyes — when their

sons go out to fight — and lose — their — lives. — I said:

Fade on last repeat

Additional Lyrics

2. War, uh! What is it good for? Absolutely nothing; say it again;
   War, uh! What is it good for? Absolutely nothing.
   War, it ain't nothing but a heartbreaker;
   War, friend only to the undertaker.
   War is an enemy to all mankind.
   The thought of war blows my mind.
   War has caused unrest within the younger generation;
   Induction then destruction, who wants to die? Ah

3. War, uh um; What is it good for? You tell me nothing, um!
   War, uh! What is it good for? Absolutely nothing.
   Good God, war, it's nothing but a heartbreaker;
   War, friend only to the undertaker.
   Wars have shattered many a young man's dreams;
   Made him disabled, bitter and mean.
   Life is much too short and precious to spend fighting wars each day.
   War can't give life, it can only take it away. Ah

4. War, Uh um! What is it good for? Absolutely nothing, um.
   War, good God almighty, listen, what is it good for? Absolutely nothing, yeah.
   War, it ain't nothing but a heartbreaker;
   War, friend only to the undertaker.
   Peace, love and understanding,
   Tell me is there no place for them today?
   They say we must fight to keep our freedom,
   But Lord knows it's gotta be a better way.

5. I say war, uh um, yeah, yeah. What is it good for? Absolutely nothing; say it again;
   War, yea, yea, yea, yea, what is it good for? Absolutely nothing; say it again;
   War, nothing but a heartbreaker; What is it good for? Friend only to the undertaker....
   (Fade)

WE SHALL OVERCOME

Musical and Lyrical Adaptation by ZILPHIA HORTON,
FRANK HAMILTON, GUY CARAWAN and PETE SEEGER
Inspired by African American Gospel Singing, members of the Food and Tobacco
Workers Union, Charleston, SC, and the southern Civil Rights Movement

Moderately slow, with determination

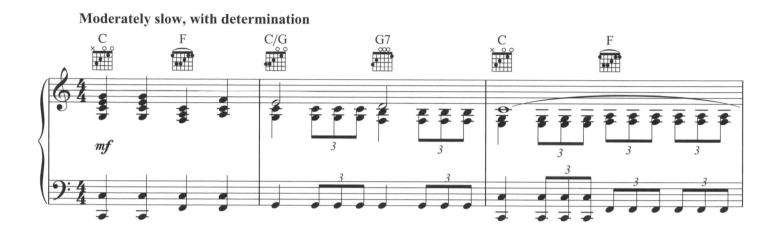

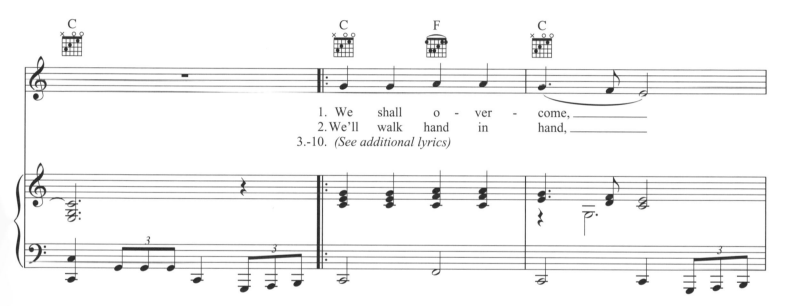

1. We shall o - ver - come, _____
2. We'll walk hand in hand, _____
3.-10. *(See additional lyrics)*

we shall o - ver - come, _____ we shall o - ver -
we'll walk hand in hand, _____ we'll walk hand in

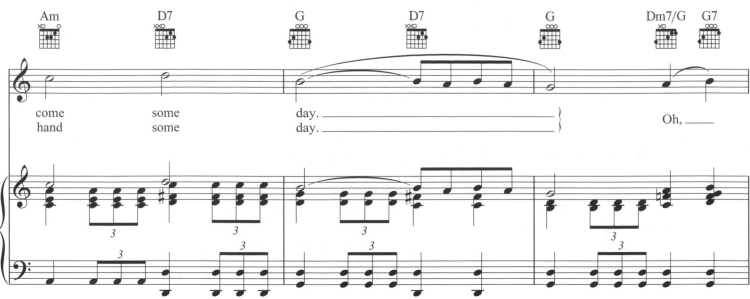

come some day. _____ Oh, _____
hand some some day. _____

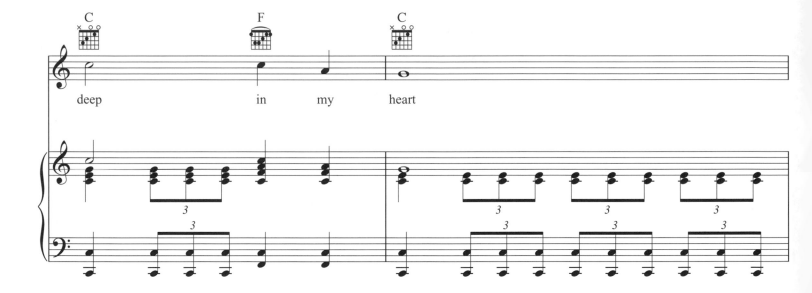

deep in my heart

I do be - lieve we shall o - ver -

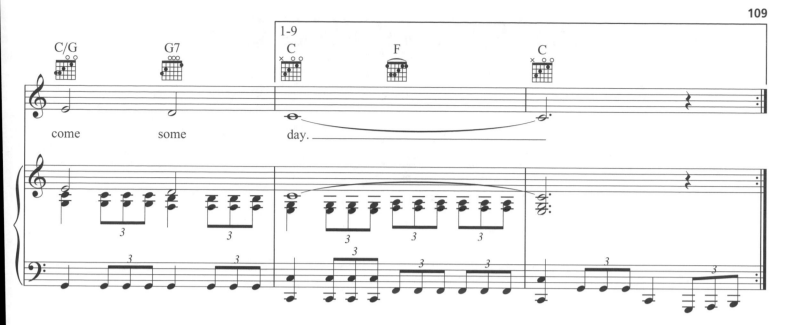

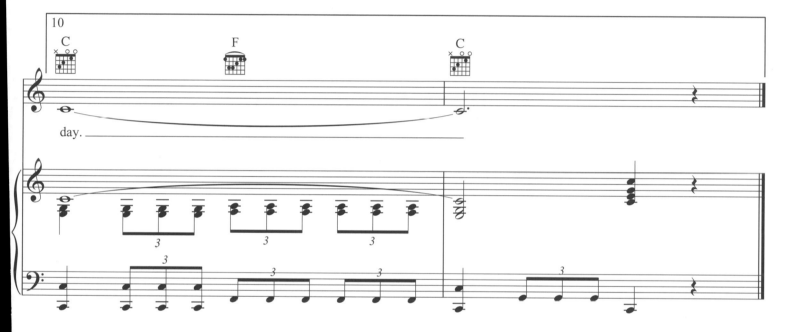

Additional Lyrics

3. We are not afraid, we are not afraid,
   We are not afraid today.
   Oh, deep in my heart I do believe
   We shall overcome some day.

4. We shall stand together, we shall stand together,
   We shall stand together now.
   Oh, deep in my heart I do believe
   We shall overcome some day.

5. The truth will make us free, the truth will make us free,
   The truth will make us free some day.
   Oh, deep in my heart I do believe
   We shall overcome some day.

6. The Lord will see us through, the Lord will see us through,
   The Lord will see us through some day.
   Oh, deep in my heart I do believe
   We shall overcome some day.

7. We shall be like Him, we shall be like Him,
   We shall be like Him some day.
   Oh, deep in my heart I do believe
   We shall overcome some day.

8. We shall live in peace, we shall live in peace,
   We shall live in peace some day.
   Oh, deep in my heart I do believe
   We shall overcome some day.

9. The whole wide world around, the whole wide world around,
   The whole wide world around some day.
   Oh, deep in my heart I do believe
   We shall overcome some day.

10. We shall overcome, we shall overcome,
    We shall overcome some day.
    Oh, deep in my heart I do believe
    We shall overcome some day.

WHAT'S GOING ON

Words and Music by RENALDO BENSON,
ALFRED CLEVELAND and MARVIN GAYE

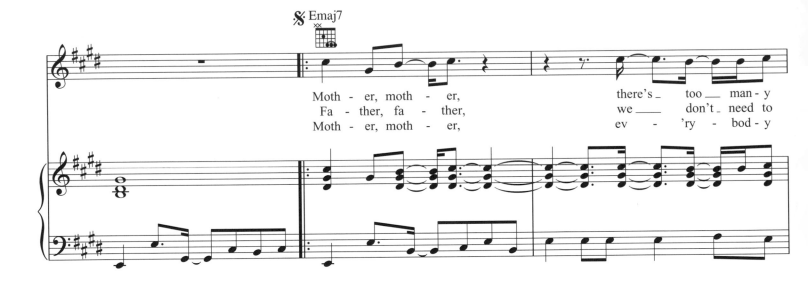

Mother, moth - er,   there's   too _ man - y
Fa - ther, fa - ther,   we _   don't need to
Moth - er, moth - er,   ev - 'ry - bod - y

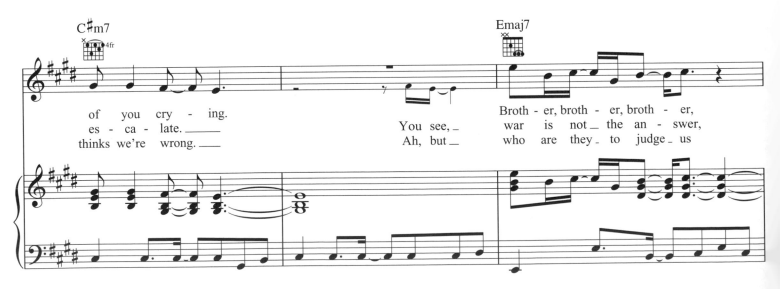

of you cry - ing.   Broth - er, broth - er, broth - er,
es - ca - late. _____   You see, _   war is not _ the an - swer,
thinks we're wrong. _____ Ah, but _   who are they _ to judge _ us

there's far too man-y of you__ dy - ing.
for on - ly love can con - quer__ hate. _____
sim - ply 'cause our hair is __ long. _____

You __ know __ we've got to find __ a way __ to bring some
You __ know __ we've got to find __ a way __ to bring some
Ah, you know __ we've got to find __ a way __ to bring some un - der -

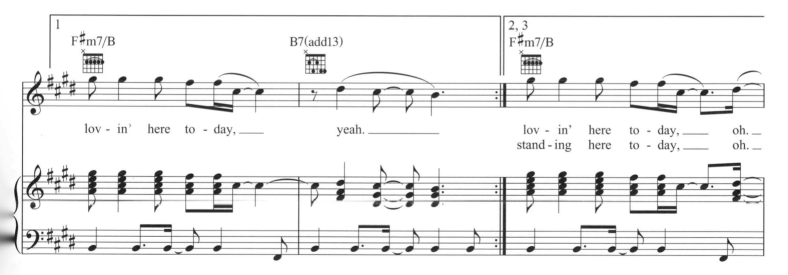

lov - in' here to - day, ____ yeah. _____ lov - in' here to - day, ____ oh. ____
stand - ing here to - day, ____ oh. ____

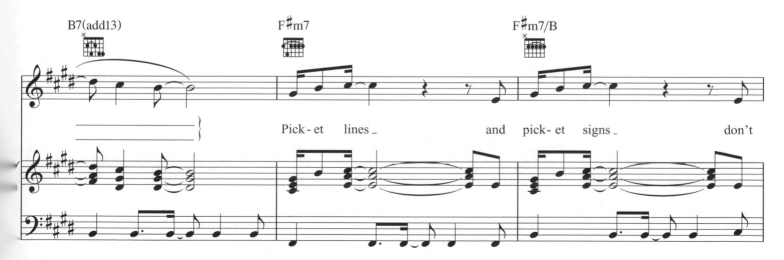

_____ Pick - et lines __ and pick - et signs __ don't

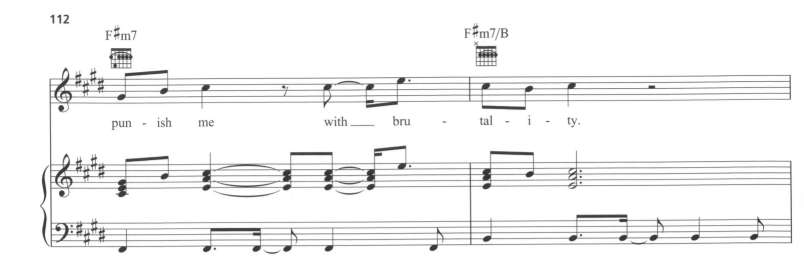

ah, ah.

I, ___ yi, yi, yi, ___ yi, yi, ___ yi, ya, ___ ya, ya, ___ ya.

I, ___ yi, yi, ___ yi, yi, ___ yi, ya, ___ ya, ya, ___ ya, ya. ___

A/B

Be, doot, de doot; Be, be, be, doot; Be be, be, doot;

D.S. al Coda
(take 2nd ending)

Bu, doot, be, be, be, doot; Be be, be, be, be, doot.

CODA

C#m7

Am9

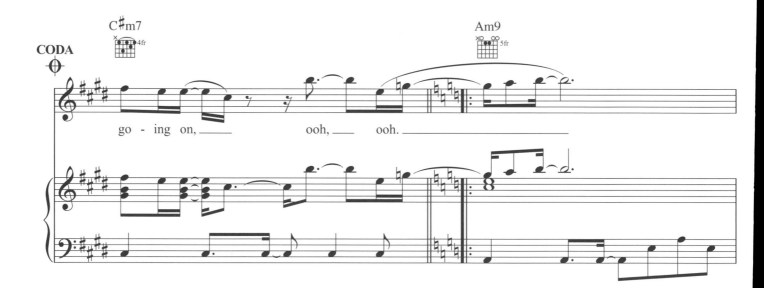

go - ing on, ooh, ooh.

I, yi, yi, yi, yi, yi, yi, ya,

ya, ya, ya.

I, yi, yi, yi, yi, yi, ya, ya, ya, ya, ya.

A/B

Be, doot, de, doot; Be, be, be, doot; Be, be, be, doot;

Repeat and Fade

Bu, doot, be, be, be, doot; Be, be, be, be, be, doot. Ooh.

WHERE HAVE ALL THE FLOWERS GONE?

Words and Music by
PETE SEEGER

1. Where have all the flow-ers gone? Long time pass-ing.
3., 5. *(See additional lyrics)*

Where have all the flow-ers gone? Long time a - go.

Where have all the flow-ers gone? The girls have picked them, ev - 'ry one.

Additional Lyrics

3. Where have all the young men gone? Long time passing.
Where have all the young men gone? Long time ago.
Where have all the young men gone?
They're all in uniform.
Oh, when will they ever learn?
Oh, when will they ever learn?

4. Where have all the soldiers gone? Long time passing.
Where have all the soldiers gone? Long time ago.
Where have all the soldiers gone?
They've gone to graveyards, every one.
Oh, when will they ever learn?
Oh, when will they ever learn?

5. Where have all the graveyards gone? Long time passing.
Where have all the graveyards gone? Long time ago.
Where have all the graveyards gone?
They're covered with flowers, every one.
Oh, when will they ever learn?
Oh, when will they ever learn?

6. Where have all the flowers gone? Long time passing.
Where have all the flowers gone? Long time ago.
Where have all the flowerss gone?
Young girls picked them, every one.
Oh, when will they ever learn?
Oh, when will they ever learn?

BIG BOOKS of Music

Our "Big Books" feature big selections of popular titles under one cover, perfect for performing musicians, music aficionados or the serious hobbyist. All books are arranged for piano, voice, and guitar, and feature stay-open binding, so the books lie flat without breaking the spine.

BIG BOOK OF BALLADS – 2ND ED.
62 songs.
00310485 .... $19.95

BIG BOOK OF BIG BAND HITS
84 songs.
00310701 .... $22.99

BIG BOOK OF BLUEGRASS SONGS
70 songs.
00311484 .... $19.95

BIG BOOK OF BLUES
80 songs.
00311843 .... $19.99

BIG BOOK OF BROADWAY
70 songs.
00311658 .... $19.99

BIG BOOK OF CHILDREN'S SONGS
55 songs.
00359261 .... $16.99

GREAT BIG BOOK OF CHILDREN'S SONGS
76 songs.
00510002 .... $15.99

FANTASTIC BIG BOOK OF CHILDREN'S SONGS
66 songs.
00311062 .... $17.95

BIG BOOK OF CHRISTMAS SONGS – 2ND ED.
126 songs.
00311520 .... $19.95

BIG BOOK OF CLASSICAL MUSIC
100 songs.
00310508 .... $19.99

BIG BOOK OF CONTEMPORARY CHRISTIAN FAVORITES – 3RD ED.
50 songs.
00312067 .... $21.99

BIG BOOK OF '50s & '60s SWINGING SONGS
67 songs.
00310982 .... $19.95

BIG BOOK OF FOLKSONGS
125 songs.
00312549 .... $19.99

BIG BOOK OF FRENCH SONGS
70 songs.
00311154 .... $19.95

BIG BOOK OF GERMAN SONGS
78 songs.
00311816 .... $19.99

BIG BOOK OF GOSPEL SONGS
100 songs.
00310604 .... $19.95

BIG BOOK OF HYMNS
125 hymns.
00310510 .... $19.99

BIG BOOK OF IRISH SONGS
76 songs.
00510981 .... $19.99

BIG BOOK OF ITALIAN FAVORITES
80 songs.
00311185 .... $19.99

BIG BOOK OF JAZZ – 2ND ED.
75 songs.
00311557 .... $22.99

BIG BOOK OF LATIN AMERICAN SONGS
89 songs.
00311562 .... $19.95

BIG BOOK OF LOVE SONGS
80 songs.
00310784 .... $19.95

BIG BOOK OF MOTOWN
84 songs.
00311061 .... $19.95

BIG BOOK OF MOVIE MUSIC
72 songs.
00311582 .... $19.95

BIG BOOK OF NOSTALGIA
158 songs.
00310004 .... $24.99

BIG BOOK OF OLDIES
73 songs.
00310756 .... $19.95

THE BIG BOOK OF PRAISE & WORSHIP
52 songs.
00140795 .... $22.99

BIG BOOK OF RAGTIME PIANO
63 songs.
00311749 .... $19.95

BIG BOOK OF ROCK
78 songs.
00311566 .... $22.95

BIG BOOK OF SOUL
71 songs.
00510771 .... $19.95

BIG BOOK OF STANDARDS
86 songs.
00311667 .... $19.95

BIG BOOK OF SWING
84 songs.
00310359 .... $19.95

BIG BOOK OF TORCH SONGS – 2ND ED.
75 songs.
00310561 .... $19.99

BIG BOOK OF TV THEME SONGS
78 songs.
00310504 .... $19.95

BIG BOOK OF WEDDING MUSIC
77 songs.
00311567 .... $22.99

THE NEW DECADE SERIES

Books with Online Audio • Arranged for Piano, Voice, and Guitar

The New Decade Series features collections of iconic songs from each decade with great backing tracks so you can play them and sound like a pro. You access the tracks online for streaming or download. **See complete song listings online at www.halleonard.com**

SONGS OF THE 1920s

Ain't Misbehavin' • Baby Face • California, Here I Come • Fascinating Rhythm • I Wanna Be Loved by You • It Had to Be You • Mack the Knife • Ol' Man River • Puttin' on the Ritz • Rhapsody in Blue • Someone to Watch over Me • Tea for Two • Who's Sorry Now • and more.
00137576 P/V/G...................................$24.99

SONGS OF THE 1930s

As Time Goes By • Blue Moon • Cheek to Cheek • Embraceable You • A Fine Romance • Georgia on My Mind • I Only Have Eyes for You • The Lady Is a Tramp • On the Sunny Side of the Street • Over the Rainbow • Pennies from Heaven • Stormy Weather (Keeps Rainin' All the Time) • The Way You Look Tonight • and more.
00137579 P/V/G...................................$24.99

SONGS OF THE 1940s

At Last • Boogie Woogie Bugle Boy • Don't Get Around Much Anymore • God Bless' the Child • How High the Moon • It Could Happen to You • La Vie En Rose (Take Me to Your Heart Again) • Route 66 • Sentimental Journey • The Trolley Song • You'd Be So Nice to Come Home To • Zip-A-Dee-Doo-Dah • and more.
00137582 P/V/G...................................$24.99

SONGS OF THE 1950s

Ain't That a Shame • Be-Bop-A-Lula • Chantilly Lace • Earth Angel • Fever • Great Balls of Fire • Love Me Tender • Mona Lisa • Peggy Sue • Que Sera, Sera (Whatever Will Be, Will Be) • Rock Around the Clock • Sixteen Tons • A Teenager in Love • That'll Be the Day • Unchained Melody • Volare • You Send Me • Your Cheatin' Heart • and more.
00137595 P/V/G...................................$24.99

SONGS OF THE 1960s

All You Need Is Love • Beyond the Sea • Born to Be Wild • California Girls • Dancing in the Street • Happy Together • King of the Road • Leaving on a Jet Plane • Louie, Louie • My Generation • Oh, Pretty Woman • Sunshine of Your Love • Under the Boardwalk • You Really Got Me • and more.
00137596 P/V/G $24.99

SONGS OF THE 1970s

ABC • Bridge over Troubled Water • Cat's in the Cradle • Dancing Queen • Free Bird • Goodbye Yellow Brick Road • Hotel California • I Will Survive • Joy to the World • Killing Me Softly with His Song • Layla • Let It Be • Piano Man • The Rainbow Connection • Stairway to Heaven • The Way We Were • Your Song • and more.
00137599 P/V/G $27.99

SONGS OF THE 1980s

Addicted to Love • Beat It • Careless Whisper • Come on Eileen • Don't Stop Believin' • Every Rose Has Its Thorn • Footloose • I Just Called to Say I Love You • Jessie's Girl • Livin' on a Prayer • Saving All My Love for You • Take on Me • Up Where We Belong • The Wind Beneath My Wings • and more.
00137600 P/V/G $27.99

SONGS OF THE 1990s

Angel • Black Velvet • Can You Feel the Love Tonight • (Everything I Do) I Do It for You • Friends in Low Places • Hero • I Will Always Love You • More Than Words • My Heart Will Go On (Love Theme from 'Titanic') • Smells like Teen Spirit • Under the Bridge • Vision of Love • Wonderwall • and more.
00137601 P/V/G $27.99

SONGS OF THE 2000s

Bad Day • Beautiful • Before He Cheats • Chasing Cars • Chasing Pavements • Drops of Jupiter (Tell Me) • Fireflies • Hey There Delilah • How to Save a Life • I Gotta Feeling • I'm Yours • Just Dance • Love Story • 100 Years • Rehab • Unwritten • You Raise Me Up • and more.
00137608 P/V/G $27.99

SONGS OF THE 2010S

All About That Bass • All of Me • Brave • Empire State of Mind • Get Lucky • Happy • Hey, Soul Sister • I Knew You Were Trouble • Just the Way You Are • Need You Now • Pompeii • Radioactive • Rolling in the Deep • Shake It Off • Shut up and Dance • Stay with Me • Take Me to Church • Thinking Out Loud • Uptown Funk • and many more.
00151836 P/V/G $27.99

halleonard.com
Prices, content, and availability
subject to change without notice.